with thanks

Antony

Antony's Private Parts

Antony as Baptista in The Taming of the Shrew

Antony's Private Parts

James Hawkins

*A peek behind the curtain at one of
the world's longest running theatrical icons...
Antony Holland*

Bliss Publications – Gabriola Island, BC, Canada

Antony's Private Parts

Copyright © James Hawkins 2011

Canadian Cataloguing in Publication Data
Hawkins, (Derek) James, 1947 –
Title - Antony's Private Parts

ISBN   Hardcover 1st edition _ 978-0-9877852-0-6
           Paperback edition _ 978-0-9877852-1-3

Biography
1. Holland, Antony. 2 Theatre, Canada. 3 Theatre, WWII, North Africa Campaign. 4 Bristol Old Vic. Theatre. 5. Studio 58, Langara College.

Published in Canada by:
        Bliss Publications
        Gabriola Island
        British Columbia, V0R 1X1
        email: gabriolablisspublications@yahoo.ca

Printed and bound in Victoria, Canada by Printorium Bookworks
www.islandblue.com

Hardcover - Limited first edition – December 2011
Perfect-bound paper edition – May 2012

Typeset in Palatino Linotype

Cover illustration: "Antony at 91" by Leslie Parrott

Author's website:www.thefishkisser.com

Table of Contents

Foreword by Christopher Gaze
Performance Notes
Acknowledgements
Prologue by William Shakespeare

Foreword

It was back in the mid 1980's that I first caught sight of Antony. He had just completed his brilliant Artistic Directorship of Studio 58 at Langara College. He had nurtured the school since its creation and was moving onto the next stage of his long and extraordinary life.

I share a similar heritage to Antony – he taught for a decade at a great British theatrical institution, the Bristol Old Vic Theatre School – beginning there in the forties. I went there as a student from 1970 -1973. Antony is from the West Country in the UK – my family moved there when I went off to theatre school.

I share Antony's passion to encourage young talent and to stay deeply connected to the theatre family that we love. But to replicate Antony's staggering accomplishments is simply not possible – as Lear says "we that are young shall never see so much, nor live so long." I am no longer young of course but to continue producing, presenting and running theatres as I advance ever onwards into my nineties…well, we'll see.

Antony trod our Bard boards in 2005 – naturally he played Adam in "As You Like It." I had played it the two previous times, I was ridiculously young – and now here was the real thing, played infinitely better! Best of all – he really was four score – he was everything described in Adam's exquisite speech about love, loyalty and courage:

> "Let me be your servant:
> Though I look old, yet I am strong and lusty;
> For in my youth I never did apply
> Hot and rebellious liquors in my blood,
> Nor did not with unbashful forehead woo
> The means of weakness and debility;
> Therefore my age is as a lusty winter,
> Frosty, but kindly: let me go with you;
> I'll do the service of a younger man
> In all your business and necessities.

He was the model of an actor during his Bard summer – he arrived promptly in his Smart car – he made his entrances with his usual flare and he was a witty and warm presence in the dressing room among his good companions in the Bard Company.

I am honoured to write these words in recognition of a great man of the theatre and a treasured friend. I marvel at Antony's magnificent contribution to our community and to the theatre in Canada. He has steadfastly served the theatre. He has given his all, never for personal gain but all for the good, all for the betterment of everything we strive to accomplish.

As I write, I seem to hear Antony's voice – is it Lear, Prospero? No it's Hamlet's:

"There is special providence in the fall of a sparrow. If it be now, 'tis not to come; if it be not to come, it will be now; if it be not now, yet it will come — the readiness is all."

Antony is always ready to put on another play, to offer encouragement and to serve the theatre – are you?

On behalf of the theatre family whom you love and who love you, Antony – we salute you and your wonderful life. Thank you m'dear!

With great affection

Christopher Grace

Performance Notes

This book is dedicated to my long-suffering wife, Sheila Swanson, who not only tolerated being a writer's-widow for the two years that it took to create this work, but was also the chief researcher, editor, fact-checker, coffee-maker and proofreader throughout the process. Additionally, I would like to offer my heartiest thanks to William Shakespeare for so often putting into words the sentiments I wanted to express.

**"The Complete Works of Antony Holland"** would fill a weighty tome, but, to misquote Blaise Pascal, I made time to write a short one. And, as Shakespeare's Othello says, "By your gracious patience I will a round unvarnish'd tale deliver."

"All the world's a stage," and Antony Holland has strutted upon it for the past ninety one years as an actor, director and teacher. He is an inspirational character _sans pareil_ whose life's story involves many well-known theatrical personalities. It is peppered with pathos, humour, intrigues and sexual missteps, and his epitaph could be taken from the words of another great Antony – Shakespeare's Antony in _Julius Caesar_:

> His life was gentle, and the elements so mix'd in him
> That Nature might stand up
> And say to the world, "This was a man!"

James Hawkins

Author's Note: Should you be wondering: Antony Holland did not write the many letters that are scattered throughout this book. However, all of the missives are substantively true in content and could have been contemporaneously penned by him.

Acknowledgements

I would like to thank the following for their assistance in making this production possible:

Canadian Cast and Crew:

Layla Alizada
Tony Bancroft
Michael Bawtree
John Braithwaite
Jonathon Bryden
Catherine Cains (K. Summers)
Shawne Davidson
Christopher Gaze
Lara Gilchrist
Lynna Goldhar
Denise Golemblaski
Jane Heyman
Gusta Holland (née Harman)
Rosheen Holland
Jasmine Howes
Maysie Hoy (Marlett)
Roy Innes
Mike Mathews
Prudence Olenik
Tyler Page
Leslie Parrott
Nick Rice
Suzanne Ristic
Audrey Sumner
J. Peter Stein
Dirk Van Stralen
Denyse Wilson
Susan Yates

United Kingdom Cast and Crew

Gillian Beton
Dorothy Gunn (née Colebrook)
Douglas Kaye Don Holland
Irene Holland
Lisa Hoghton
Lord Victor Killearn
Phyllida Law
Alban Morley
Alistair Murphy
Kerry Shale

Channel Islands:
Research assistant:
Christine Lloyd

Egypt:
Research assistant:
Noura Bahgat

Legal Services (Can):
Diane Cornish

Audio recordings:
Patsy Ludwick

Cover Design:
Leslie Parrott

Special Thanks for Guest Appearances...

To: Bruce Mason for his rendition of "Antony Holland – A Star Turn on Gabriola Island."

To: Leslie Parrott for "Antony – The Man."

To: Shirley Brown for kindly granting permission to quote from her book: *Bristol Old Vic Theatre School – the first 50 years*

Finally – Last but not least:

Accolades to all those whose anecdotes and comments about Antony ended up on the cutting room floor. Sorry folks - that's showbiz!

Prologue
by
William Shakespeare

All the world's a stage,
And all the men and women merely players:
They have their exits and their entrances;
And one man in his time plays many parts,
His acts being seven ages. At first the infant,
Mewling and puking in the nurse's arms.
And then the whining school-boy, with his satchel
And shining morning face, creeping like snail
Unwillingly to school. And then the lover,
Sighing like furnace, with a woeful ballad
Made to his mistress' eyebrow. Then a soldier,
Full of strange oaths and bearded like the pard,
Jealous in honour, sudden and quick in quarrel,
Seeking the bubble reputation
Even in the cannon's mouth. And then the justice,
In fair round belly with good capon lined,
With eyes severe and beard of formal cut,
Full of wise saws and modern instances;
And so he plays his part. The sixth age shifts
Into the lean and slipper'd pantaloon,
With spectacles on nose and pouch on side,
His youthful hose, well saved, a world too wide
For his shrunk shank; and his big manly voice,
Turning again toward childish treble, pipes
And whistles in his sound. Last scene of all,
That ends this strange eventful history,
Is second childishness and mere oblivion,
Sans teeth, sans eyes, sans taste, sans everything.

(As You Like It)

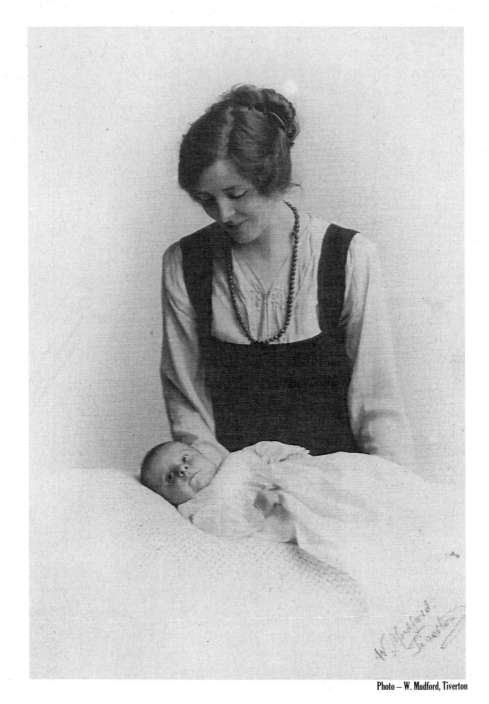

Photo – W. Mudford, Tiverton

Beatrice Holland and first born son, Albert Edwin – 1920

Antony's Private Parts

Overture

*When we are born, we cry that we are come
To this great stage of fools:*
                              (Shak. King Lear)

The Roaring Twenties was a colourful period sandwiched between the hardships of the First World War and the Great Depression of the late twenties. Fifteen million people had been killed in the so-called 'War to end all wars' and as many as one hundred million had died, worldwide, in the Spanish Flu pandemic that followed it.

By the beginning of the 1920s people around the globe were longing for better times and there was a feeling of great exuberance as a new age dawned. This was the age of Dixieland Jazz and Flappers: of affordable cars, radios and gramophones: of talkies and transatlantic airships: of art nouveau and of women suffragettes. It was in many ways the very beginning of the 'Modern Era'. However, times of upheaval inevitably create losers as well as winners and, with the development of radio and cinema (and eventually television), the golden age of British theatre was coming to an end.

The gradual decline of live performance in the first few decades of the twentieth century had little impact on the ten thousand inhabitants of the peaceful town of Tiverton in the West of England. This ancient settlement, in the heart of the pastoral county of Devon, was a blue-collar community of farmers and mill workers in the early 1900s and had no professional theatre. Touring repertory companies occasionally visited the town but James Mason, *(1909 – 1984)*, one of Britain's most acclaimed actors, wrote in his autobiography that the town was notorious for its theatre audiences… because they never showed up.

Britain had been at the forefront of dramatic theatre since the reign of Queen Elizabeth I when William Shakespeare, Ben Jonson, Christopher Marlowe, and many others had entertained the masses, but a new and progressive age demanded novel forms of entertainment and, with the arrival of motion pictures, actors from all over the world were quitting the stage and flocking to Hollywood to seek fame and fortune on the silver screen.

Audiences were entranced by the antics of Charlie Chaplin and the Keystone Kops, along with the glamorous images of stars like Mary Pickford and Rudolph Valentino, and millions sought respite from their humdrum lives in the smoke-filled cinemas that were springing up in towns and cities around the world. The Electric Palace cinema in Tiverton was one such venue, and it was here that George Holland met Beatrice Green in January of 1919 and set in motion the events that would ultimately fill the pages of this book.

Edwin Holland, universally known as George, was big and brusque; a burly ex-soldier with a nasal Birmingham accent and a passion for motor racing, beer and beautiful women. He was an amateur race driver who would later name two of his children after great racers of the day: Donald Campbell and Kaye Don.

Beatrice Green was just one of George's loves. She was a beautiful redhead and is reputed to have looked exactly like a young Eleanor Roosevelt. She came from Oakford, near Tiverton, and was the daughter of Sidney Green, a carpenter who hailed from Guernsey in the Channel Islands where he had been gardener to the famous French writer, Victor Hugo. During the War Beatrice had been a Land Army girl, but when she and George met she was working in a parachute factory in Bristol. She had been visiting her home in Oakford when they fell in love in the Electric Palace cinema in Tiverton.

In 1919, with the 'War to end all wars' finally over, George took off his uniform to follow his passion for motoring and, with some assistance from the Heathcoat family, the local mill owners, opened a garage next to their mill in the West-Exe district of Tiverton. He then followed his passion for women by marrying Beatrice.

Beatrice was from an ordinary, fairly poor, family, but now that she was a businessman's wife she quickly became sophisticated, even posh by rural Devonian standards. She was reputed to be a 'real lady', (though, as we will discover, she was not quite the lady she might have aspired to be).

George was a man of his time; a stern disciplinarian who had soldiered through the First World War in the trenches of France and now ruled his household with a patriarchal fist, but this is not his story. This is the story of Albert, his eldest son, born on March 28, 1920, who was destined to become Antony Holland: actor, director, mentor, and an influential figure on the Canadian stage.

According to Shakespeare, *'One man in his time plays many parts'*. Few men play as many parts in their lives as Antony Holland, both in and out of the public eye, and this book is a record of both his very public and very private parts.

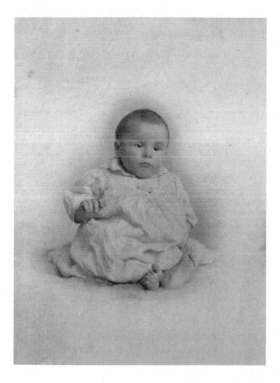

Antony — Aged 9 months

Act 1

The Early Years

At first the infant,
Mewling and puking in the nurse's arms.
And then the whining school-boy, with his satchel
And shining morning face, creeping like snail
Unwillingly to school.

(Shak. As You Like It)

George and Beatrice Holland's first child was a sensitive, creative boy who would develop little interest in the macho world of motor sports as he grew, and was therefore destined to become a great disappointment to his father. "I was frightened of my father," Antony readily admits today, and he was not alone in that fear within the family. Although little is known of Antony's early life he was not regarded as a particularly strong child and nearly died of pneumonia at eighteen months. His seemingly miraculous recovery was attributed to a jar of jellied meats a well-wisher with Wicca powers had given to his mother.

Beatrice Holland had conflicting beliefs in both the spiritual and the occult and, to Antony's recollection, she changed religions as often as she changed coats. But, whatever the religion of the month, Beatrice believed in the supernatural. She would visit a clairvoyant in the nearby city of Exeter and young Antony would wait downstairs while the two women went upstairs to consult. One day the clairvoyant came down with his mother and stared at him for a long time before declaring, "He will command great crowds one day".

At the age of three, Antony went to Heathcoat Infant School where he learned to write with chalk on a slate. The school was named after John Heathcoat, a businessman who had brought lace making to Tiverton in 1816 after Luddites smashed his patented lace making machines in Loughborough in the English Midlands. When Antony was a child, before the Great Depression, lace making was the main industry in Tiverton, after farming, and the Heathcoat family still owned most of the factories and town buildings.

One person who had a significant influence on young Antony's life was Sidney Green, his grandfather. Granddad Green, as he was known to Antony and his siblings, was a kindly man with a bushy beard who made bows and arrows for the boys and told risqué tales about Victor Hugo running naked around the grounds of his Guernsey house. Sidney's home in nearby Oakford was a warm and welcoming country cottage which he shared with two of his adult daughters (Antony's aunts), Ilma and Olive. Here the young Holland brothers could feed the chickens and ducks, eat apples in the orchard, and play freely in the surrounding fields.

Life at home with an overbearing father was less idyllic for Antony, although George's infatuation with cars and women, and his love of a 'good pint', meant that he was often out of the house. His mother, Beatrice, regularly worked in the office at the garage, so Antony and his brothers were frequently left in the care of Winifred, a live-in maid, and would spend their free time playing in and around the mill stream, a tributary of the River Exe known as The Leat (often brightly coloured with dye from the nearby mill) that ran behind their father's garage. However, while his siblings engaged in the rough and tumble of boyhood games and sports, Antony preferred to practice the gentler arts of singing and acting.

Antony could read, write and do basic mathematics by age five and he graduated to Heathcoat Boys' School at age seven. By the time he was eight or nine he was already a regular performer – putting on a one-boy variety show for small audiences of his peers. He would sing popular songs with actions, and perform self-written sketches and fashionable skits of the day. And (and this will come as no surprise to anyone who has ever known Antony) he would always charge an admission fee for his shows; either a ha'penny or a penny, though he would never cheapen himself by accepting a farthing!

English was Antony's best subject at school and he loved writing essays. He always insisted on perfect handwriting and would spend days on each piece: the teacher was indulgent, knowing that he would do a good job while other students were fast but sloppy. Alternatively, Antony was not good at woodwork and would spend all year fashioning something simple like a pencil box when everyone else made many more elaborate objects.

Antony's early acting career really took off when he played the Magistrate in Dickens' *Oliver Twist* at school. For this role he had to portray old age – something he still hasn't mastered today at the age of ninety one – but he did it so well he was commended. "Everyone said I was great," he explains, so when the next play came along he was sadly disappointed when he was given a non-speaking role as a pirate.

While frequent disappointment is an actor's lot, it is a hard lesson to learn at the age of ten. So, in recompense, Beatrice took Antony to see plays such as *The Curtain Call* and *She Stoops to Conquer* at The Theatre Royal in Exeter, where he was able to absorb the atmosphere of real theatre and imagine himself onstage.

From his earliest years Antony never wavered in his determination to be an actor, and he so enjoyed performing that he was willing to join any organization that put on concerts irrespective of their political or religious leanings. He wanted to join the Scouts in order to participate in *The Gang Show* (an annual variety performance featuring talented Scouters that eventually became a revered national event), but his father stopped him because he believed the movement was militaristic. Antony rebelled by joining an equally martial organization, the Church Boys' Brigade. He was already a regular churchgoer and a choirboy at St. Paul's Anglican Church. Annual celebrations such as Christmas, Easter and the Bishop's visit, were his particular favourites because the choir would process from the vestry around the outside of the church to make a grand entrance and sweep majestically down the aisle while singing. But it wasn't a good choir; the unrehearsed and unruly young boys were generally drowned out by the women choristers and would vent their boredom by scribbling in the hymn books and carving chunks out of the ornate wooden choir stalls with penknives during the sermon.

Antony was paid two shillings a quarter which doubled to four shillings when he was finally promoted to head choirboy. However, his stardom lasted just a few months because his voice began to break and he was booted out. In any case, by this time he was becoming disillusioned with Christianity and openly questioned why a god clever enough to make elephants, humans and hummingbirds, would be silly enough to send his only son down to earth to tell the Jews that they were wrong.

Before breaking with the church completely Antony wrote his first real play, *Inspector Trent's Last Case*, to be performed by the church's Sunday school. It had twenty scenes and lasted a full fifteen minutes. And, of course, Antony cast himself in the lead role.

The annual town carnival in Tiverton gave Antony another reason to dress up. Each summer his mother organized a float promoting his father's garage and she would make costumes for her boys. But Antony could never get enough of the limelight and was willing to do anything to get onto the stage. He joined a youthful group under the umbrella of the Conservative Party. It was called The Primrose Buds and was for young members of The Primrose League – a rightwing organization with religious overtones founded by Churchill and others in 1883 and named in honour of Benjamin Disraeli who was known to love primroses. Antony was blissfully ignorant of the imperialistic aims of the group, and was happy to sing the militaristic songs so enjoyed by the right wingers even though he was already a pacifist at heart. He carried a little wooden rifle and would march and do the actions as he sang songs such as...

> *"For it's the soldiers of the King, me lads.*
> *Who've seen me lads; who've been me lads.*
> *In the fight for England's glory, lads   "*

Seeking a wider audience, as he would continue to do throughout his life, Antony next joined The Band of Hope – a temperance group with Protestant leanings. This organization was founded in 1847 and was dedicated to educating young people about the perils of alcohol and drug abuse.

Antony's only knowledge of the Band was that they held concerts – after all, it was a band – and he was delighted when he was told he could sing something at an upcoming event. He ran home excitedly and collected the score for one of his favourite pieces, but when he returned he was told that he couldn't sing it. He was dreadfully upset and had to be consoled by his mother who explained the situation: he had wanted to sing a popular song of the day with the lyrics, "Drink, drink, drink brothers, drink".

Despite his infatuation with the stage Antony still found time for boyhood high jinks: swimming in the river Exe; eeling with his friend, Jimmy, in the Leat; playing marbles, conkers and hoops in the street with his younger brothers, Kenneth, Donald and Douglas (who was always known by his second name – Kaye); and generally making a nuisance of himself in his father's garage. He also had a small garden plot at the school where he developed his lifelong love of gardening.

On Saturday afternoons Antony would go to The Electric Palace cinema in Tiverton to see silent movies. He loved dramatic serials like *The Perils of Pauline* and westerns starring Tom Mix. He particularly enjoyed courtroom dramas, both in books and movies, which led him to want to put on a wig and gown and become a lawyer – until he learned that lawyers needed a university education and had to work hard.

Boys sat on the left and girls on the right of the cinema, but in cases of disturbances, which were frequent and always created by the boys, the house lights would go up and after much booing and jeering the offending lads were made to sit in the girls' section.

Antony, like his father before him, fell in love in the Electric Palace. A young girl had caught his eye but he was too shy to approach her, so each week he would buy sweets at the shop opposite the cinema and would contrive to walk past her and 'accidentally' drop some into her lap. His strategy failed and this was destined to become the first of many unrequited love affairs.

Now, at the age of twelve, Antony was attending Heathcoat Boys' School when the English teacher introduced Shakespeare...

Schoolboy Antony, (1928)

Tiverton
September 1932

My dear Friend – You must read Shakespeare!

Laurence Olivier says that Shakespeare is the nearest thing in incarnation to the eyes of God. What more can I say? I cannot get enough of him. We did the Merchant of Venice at school and I was certain I would be chosen to play Shylock. I feel that I know Shylock. Anyway, I wanted to play Shylock because he gets to sharpen a knife and lots of other interesting stuff onstage. But Victor Trude got the role and I had to play Portia ... a girl!

"*Nay, faith, let me not play a woman; I have a beard coming*", I told the teacher, quoting from A Midsummer's Night's Dream. I thought that would impress him, but it didn't make any difference. Victor stole my part. What does he know of Shylock?

Anyway, when it came to the performance he totally overacted and turned the whole thing into a farce. "*Thus the whirligig of time brings in his revenges,*" I thought as he made an ass of himself onstage, but the more stupid he was the more the audience loved it. They laughed and laughed, and the more they laughed the more serious I became. I fear that they preferred Victor to me and I just thought of Hamlet's instructions to the players:

And let those that play your clowns speak no more than is set down for them; for there be of them that will themselves laugh, to set on some quantity of barren spectators... that's villainous, and shows a most pitiful ambition in the fool that uses it.

Comedy! Hah! That's all they understand in Tiverton. They wouldn't have laughed in Exeter – they would have called him a fool.

Noel Coward is funny. Last night there was a touring company at the New Hall doing *Private Lives* and I managed to push my way in and get hired as the prompter. They didn't pay me, but this was my big chance. But you'll never believe what happened. Thanks to my prompting we made it all right to the end of the first act, but then they accidentally launched into Act 3 at the beginning of Act 2. I didn't know where they were so I kept calling out the right lines and they just kept going with the wrong ones. The audience loved it – they just laughed and laughed. What is wrong with these people? They wouldn't have laughed in Exeter.

Albert

Although Antony may have been disappointed at being denied Shylock's role in the school play, he can still recite Portia's famous mercy speech and still does so with a broad Devonian accent as he would have done at the age of twelve.

As for his debut as a prompter: the actors could well have been unprepared on this occasion, but Tiverton was renowned as a black hole for professional theatre and at least one touring company was stranded, penniless, when the manager took off with the box office takings before the show opened.

As Antony entered his teenage years his preoccupation with the stage was an irritant to his father who fostered notions of his eldest son eventually taking over the garage business. Although he inherited a love of cars from his father, and learnt to drive at the age of twelve, Antony wasn't at all interested in being a mechanic, but his father wasn't an easy man to deal with and wouldn't tolerate insurrection. It is possible that George's wartime experiences in the trenches had an effect on his psyche and made him especially hard and stubborn. He certainly liked his drink, though perhaps no more than many men of his era, and he certainly had a reputation for womanizing and for physically abusing his wife.

Beatrice wasn't lilywhite either; she was very beautiful and was flirtatious with men. On one occasion she had an assignation with a commercial traveler in Exmouth and left Antony and his brothers to play on the beach while she spent the afternoon 'shopping' with the man. On another occasion she met up with a male friend in Bude who bought Antony's youngest brother, Kaye, a kite...simply a well-meant gift perhaps? Possibly. But the young Holland boys had deep suspicions about both of their parents.

By the summer of 1934 memories of the First World War were fading and Britons were yet to wake up to the threat posed by Hitler and fascism. The Great Depression had left its mark on Tiverton – many workers had lost their jobs in the lace mill – but West-Exe Garage under George Holland's proprietorship appeared to be thriving. Antony didn't want to go to Secondary School, and had no ambition other than to be an actor, so he reluctantly accepted an informal apprenticeship in his father's business. He was just fourteen years old so he began at the bottom with joe jobs: cleaning the engines; sweeping the floors; making tea; carrying batteries to and from the charger; and, when no one was looking, sneaking away to the garden behind the garage to pick raspberries and rehearse for his next great performance.

Beatrice Holland and sons, Antony and Kenneth, dressed for the town's carnival, (circa 1933)

The Hollands' family garage in the early 1930s

Act 2

The Ups and Downs of Teenage Passions

And then the lover,
Sighing like furnace, with a woeful ballad
Made to his mistress' eyebrow.
(Shak. As You Like It)

In 1655 Oliver Cromwell signed a charter changing Tiverton's weekly market from Monday to Tuesday so that stallholders and vendors would not have to prepare their wares on the Sabbath. Market day has been held on every Tuesday since that time and when Antony was a teenager, in the 1930s, it was the day when local farmers would come into town to sell livestock and pay their bills. One of Antony's responsibilities at his father's garage was to calculate the farmers' accounts and then add twenty percent. The farmers always complained that the bills were excessive whatever the amount, so Antony's father would take them off to the nearest pub to negotiate where, over a few beers, their bills were always reduced by twenty percent and they went home happy.

But Antony hated working in his father's garage and enrolled in evening classes at The Tiverton School of Art to learn shorthand and typing so that he could pay his way through theatre school. And, never one to miss an opportunity to perform, he persuaded the drama teacher at the school to stage an edited version of Shakespeare's *Merchant of Venice* in which he would play Shylock. Antony chose his favourite act, the trial scene, and then ruthlessly eliminated most of the other characters. There were no reviews of this performance but Antony admits that it was probably terrible. He also directed Dickens' *Christmas Carol* in the church hall in which he took the lead as Scrooge. This production was also a disaster because some of the exuberant cast members danced on the billiard table and severely damaged it.

While the stage was undoubtedly Antony's greatest love, he was a lusty handsome youth with natural urgings and he had set his heart on Madge Smith, the dentist's pretty daughter. But, despite the many hours he loitered outside her parents' house trying to glimpse her in the window, he never plucked up enough courage to knock on her door.

And then there was Beryl Andrews! Beryl was a tease whose sleeveless dresses gave alluring glimpses of her plump white breasts. Antony was certainly allured, but he trailed the pack when it came to Beryl's suitors. But romance would have to take a back seat to the stage, as it would throughout most of his life. Young Antony Holland had his eyes firmly on his acting career and in his first year with the drama group at the arts school he was elected 'President'.

In late 1935 the School of Art Dramatic Society presented a one act play titled *Happy Death Ltd.* at Tiverton's New Hall Theatre. It featured Antony as a bishop. The theatre critic of the Tiverton Gazette, Michael Pertwee, reported that Mr. Holland spoke clearly with much expression and that his performance was "effective".

"Effective" was not good enough for Antony and he was happier with Pertwee's review of his next performance in a play called, *Like Will to Like*. "Holland carried the whole play along with a swing", wrote the critic, who then took the gloss off by adding, "It is no discredit to the actors when I say that, by choosing another play, they would have been more successful". But, as President of the dramatic society, Antony was on a roll and by his own admission became an insufferable dictator: he insisted on perfection, lambasted actors twice his age, and always took the best roles while mercilessly cutting other parts so that he could hog the stage.

And so it was that on Saturday, November 14, 1936, at the tender age of sixteen years, A.E.Holland, President of the Tiverton School of Art Dramatic Society, produced, directed and, naturally, starred in, his first major play at the New Hall. It was, of course, selected scenes from Shakespeare's *The Merchant of Venice*, personally chosen by Antony so that he could take the lead role of Shylock. Admission was 6 pence.

13

Tiverton School of Art Dramatic Society
request the pleasure of the attendance of

....

at a Performance of Two Plays,
Scenes from Shakespeare's Merchant of Venice
and Old Moore's Almanac (1 Act Farce)
to be given at the SCHOOL OF ART,
on SATURDAY, 14th NOVEMBER, 1936.

Curtain will rise at 8.15 p.m. sharp.   Admission 6d.

An invitation to one of Antony's early Shakespeare productions

In his determination to be in the spotlight on this occasion Antony had overextended himself and as the orchestra played the overture he was behind the curtain desperately trying to stick on his beard. When the curtain went up he was in such a state that he had completely forgotten his lines and, to the consternation of the other cast members, he walked aimlessly around the stage for several minutes before he could get both his mind and his mouth into gear.

At the time of this performance Antony was working as a shorthand typist for a law firm in Exeter by day and was also rehearsing with the Exeter Drama League for a small role in John Galsworthy's *The Silver Box* during the evenings. However, he had taken on too much and things didn't go as planned. The rehearsals ran late and he often missed the last train home to Tiverton, so he slept in his office. He was caught asleep one morning and fired from his job, and, to make matters worse, the play was roundly savaged by the critics.

Unemployed, and somewhat demoralized, Antony returned home to work in his parents' new business venture, a milk bar and café. It was preferable to working in his father's garage and gave him time to pursue both his acting and a young woman.

Mary Player was his first great love, after the stage, and they would take platonic walks together but, despite Antony's debonair façade, he was sexually naïve and was desperately seeking an opportunity to impress Mary and cement his relationship when …

Tiverton
October 25th 1937

Dear Friend

As Silvius says in As You Like It:
If thou remember'st not the slightest folly
That ever love did make thee run into,
Thou hast not lov'd:

Oh! But what folly I have run into. Her name is Mary Player... Sweet Mary Player; Divine Mary Player. Like Shakspeare's Posthumus Leonatus in Cymbeline, *I thought her as chaste as unsunn'd snow.*

But, as much as I contrived to have my way with her, I got no further than a stolen kiss and a slapped hand. And then, joy of joys, last week father went to the Motor Show at Earls Court leaving me in charge of the garage. What do I know, or care, of garage business, my mind was solely upon the sweet secret that lay 'neath Mary's knickers. As Hamlet says, *"That's a fair thought to lie between maids' legs".* And my thoughts were entirely in that direction when I hired a Hillman Minx and drove Mary to London's West End to see Gielgud in Richard II at the Queen's Theatre. Gielgud... in the flesh! How could Mary possibly deny my advances after seeing Gielgud?

What excitement... Gielgud and sexual emancipation the same night!

And there I was, waiting in the foyer of the Regent Palace Hotel in London while Mary powdered her nose, when my blasted father strolled in, saw me, stopped dead, and yelled, "What the hell are you doing here? You're supposed to be minding the bloody garage."

I withered - of all the hotels in London to choose from - and my enthusiasm for carnal enlightenment with Mary shrivelled faster than a stuck balloon. I drove straight home after the show desperately practicing Portia's speech from the Merchant - you know, the one that starts...
The quality of mercy is not strain'd,
It droppeth as the gentle rain from heaven
Upon the place beneath: It is twice blest;
It blesseth him that gives and him that takes:

I just hope my father understands Shakespeare!

Albert

P.S. I think I need a stage name - something more Shakespearean than Albert!

The course of love never did run smooth for Antony and, though he doesn't recall what lies he told his father on this occasion, his balloon had been burst and he never did discover Mary's delights. But he still has the program from the play: Gielgud, just thirty three years old and already one of the 'Greats' of British theatre, was playing the lead, backed by a dream company of twentieth century celebrities, including Peggy Ashcroft, Michael Redgrave, Anthony Quayle and Alec Guinness.

Antony must have seen something of himself in Gielgud: young, brash, ambitious and talented. Gielgud had only studied very briefly at the Royal Academy of Dramatic Art, which gave Antony hope. On the other hand, Antony judged Gielgud to be so great an actor that he considered giving up all ideas of the stage because he could never attain such a high standard. Yet, his insecurity was apparently short-lived. because a few months later the suave seventeen year old, with hair parted in the middle and a cigarette at his lips, produced a variety show at the Heathcoat Hall in Tiverton in aid of the Mayor's Xmas Fund and was sufficiently precocious to head the program with the words, 'Albert E.Holland Presents'. Imagine the audience's surprise when Albert E.Holland basically presented himself. He starred in four out of the six acts and in the opening play, *Ruined by the BBC*, he cast himself alongside Beryl Andrews, the girl whose breasts had never ceased to fascinate him.

The hall was undergoing renovation at the time and the dressing room had been demolished, leaving the cast to change outside in the cold and the audience to freeze whenever the doors were opened for the actors' entrances and exits. Antony's younger brother, Kenneth, played a very old mayor in the first scene, but he strode across the stage with such youthful exuberance that he brought the house down. But Antony's death scene from Shakespeare's *Richard II* in the final act was to be the show's *tour de force*. He had seen Gielgud's portrayal of the King's demise in London and was determined to emulate the great actor. He rehearsed repeatedly until he felt that he had mastered the moment when, after being stabbed, he would clutch his chest and cry:

"*Mount, mount my soul! thy seat is up on high:*
Whilst my gross flesh sinks downward, here to die."

He would then drop to the floor, roll dramatically toward the footlights and stop dead at the edge of the stage, with bulging eyes and protruding tongue, just inches from the audience. But he'd never tried it in costume. He had been so busy organizing everything and performing in everything that it was only at the dress rehearsal that he discovered that his wig didn't fit properly and would inevitably fall off. He considered clutching his head rather than his chest, but whom, in Shakespeare, gets stabbed in the head? He tried desperately, but nothing worked and he stomped about the stage in fury. Francis Trigger, the exasperated stage manager, was overheard saying, "If he doesn't stop soon I'll get a hammer and nail the damn thing to his skull".

Antony was finally forced to abandon his plans for a dramatic dénouement and the show fizzled in something of an anticlimax when Richard II uttered those immortal words, slipped slowly to the floor, and died peacefully on the spot.

The reviews glowed with praise for Antony, saying that he proved to be head and shoulders above the rest of the company and that he gave an excellent and skilful performance in Shakespearean scenes. There was no mention of Beryl Andrews and Antony never did get his hands on her breasts.

**Antony as Richard II
(November 1937)**

Photo - Anon

Photo – Chandler of Exeter

Portrait of Antony aged 17, (still signing himself Albert)

It was April 1938 when Antony became the drama critic for the local newspaper, the Tiverton Gazette. He was just eighteen years old and he infuriated many readers with his penned assassinations of enthusiastic, well-meaning, amateurs …

Tiverton
April 1938

Dear Friend

Great news – I'm now the <u>official</u> theatre critic at the Tiverton Gazette. As you might imagine, some people can't take the truth and there were some pretty vitriolic letters to the editor after my first reviews, so I wrote back and said that amateurs were presumptuous in assuming they knew anything about acting and that it's up to the press to disillusion those blinded by their own conceit, then perhaps their dabblings in acting will be done in more of a spirit of humility and respect.

Hah! That should shake 'em up a bit I thought, and I added ... and I quote here, *"...there is nothing more revolting to me than an amateur who thinks he is a good actor, and doesn't hesitate to say so. These misguided people should be banned from the stage. Amateurs must realize that however much talent they possess, they cannot become even competent actors, without arduous training and years of experience."*

Let's see what they think of that, I said to myself, and would you believe that some know-it-all calling himself "Frankly Disgusted of Tiverton" had the cheek to write back and say I wasn't so bloomin' good myself. Honestly!

By the way, to prove my point, can you believe what happened last week? What a farce! I was performing selected scenes from Shakespeare with some amateurs and they were still putting up the lights when the audience came in. Then, at the last minute, the girl playing Portia wanted a prompter, so I got an eager volunteer and sat her behind the curtain with a flashlight. But the stupid girl didn't know anything about acting – every time I paused for dramatic effect she leapt in with a prompt. I had to race through the piece to keep her quiet, but this so unsettled poor Portia that she got stage fright, jumped three pages of script and cut the trial scene in half. Of course, the prompter had no idea where we were and left us to muddle our way through to the end. Then the electrician forgot to turn up the house lights and we took our final bow in total darkness – which is probably why the girl who was supposed to present me with cigarettes and Portia with chocolates got confused. Anyway, I was just trying to get my ciggies back from Portia when the main curtain rod snapped and the whole lot collapsed and completely smothered us.

There is nothing for it – I have to get away from these amateurs. I bet Gielgud never has these problems in London.

Antony

In the summer of 1938 Antony saw the great Edwardian actor, Bransby Williams, at the Theatre Royal in Exeter. He was so impressed with Williams' ability to change characters without leaving the stage that he wrote, asking for advice on becoming an actor. The reply was discouraging in the extreme. "Acting today", wrote Williams, "Where is it? Real actors of the real school are walking about London, hungry. Believe me the outlook is bleak. I've done it all – 40 years from Hamlet to variety and I've lost £15,000 because of the changing times".

Spurred on by such a glowing recommendation Antony applied for a scholarship at The Royal Academy of Dramatic Art (RADA) in London. He took some coaching from the drama teacher at Tiverton's prestigious public school, Blundell's, and, out of hundreds of applicants, was awarded the sole scholarship for a male student that year. It was a prodigious achievement and a dream come true. However, the Leverhulme scholarship to RADA that was awarded to Antony only covered the course fees and not living expenses, and Antony's dream quickly evaporated when he returned home and his father declared that he had perfectly good prospects in the family business and wouldn't give him a penny to ponce about on the stage. Antony's mother, who had always supported and encouraged his acting ambitions, was powerless to change his father's mind and Antony had to turn the scholarship down.

With one door closed another opened. A few weeks later Antony saw a newspaper article about a new theatre school in south London, called 'Labour Stage' which had broken away from a communist theatrical group. This evening school was to be run in an old warehouse close to where Shakespeare's plays were first performed in Southwark, and Antony would be able to pay his way by working as a stenographer for London Transport during the day. Fees were based on ability to pay, and the school attracted students from a wide range of backgrounds and disciplines whose only commonality was their absolute determination to succeed on the stage.

Nelson Illingworth, an Australian opera singer with a sadistic streak, led the school and insisted that breath control was pivotal; requiring every student to recite fourteen lines of Shakespeare without taking a second breath – which only encouraged them to speak incredibly fast. It was a three year course of dance, voice and drama, at the end of which it was hoped that the successful students would form a touring theatre group.

After three weeks on the course, Illingworth invited Antony to reprise the audition piece he had performed when he'd applied. He was very proud to be chosen and, in front of the entire school, gave his all to the role of Shylock in a scene from *The Merchant of Venice*, beginning, *"Hath not a Jew eyes..."* As he sat down Illingworth turned to the group and smugly said, "That's exactly the kind of bad acting we are here to change".

Dancing was a struggle for Antony. He had never been athletic, unlike his brother Kenneth who was an award-winning Olympian, so he hid in the back row of the dancing class until he was caught and made to dance where the instructor, Margaret Barr, could see him.

Every week each student was required to present a couple of dramatic mimes, but Antony's were just too dramatic; he was always escaping from a burning building or finding a poisonous snake in his bed. Eventually he was told to wash dishes or sew on buttons instead.

Antony's London stage debut was on April 1, 1939, when he performed at The Royal Albert Hall in a show titled *Music for the People* starring the famed American singer, Paul Robeson. Antony had the lead role in a scene of rebellion as John Ball – a fourteenth century English priest who had advocated an end to slavery. He wasn't particularly proud of his performance at the time, although he still has the program autographed by Paul Robeson.

Money was tight while Antony was at Labour Stage. At weekends he would spin out a single beer for hours so that he could sit in the warmth of a pub rather than freeze in his Pimlico bed-sit that was heated by a single gas ring. He would try to afford one hot meal a day and his mother sent food parcels. She also gave him a golden guinea for emergencies, which he never spent, although he pawned his Parker fountain pen on one occasion when he was desperate. Later, after a spell sharing a room in Blackfriars with an unemployed writer who made awful meals with vegetables discarded from the market, Antony took a room near St. Paul's Cathedral with an Irish woman, Rosheen Napier, who was the 'mother' of the group at Labour Stage. She even had a shower – and took cold showers in the belief that it was good for her.

Antony eventually left London Transport when overtime interfered with his studies, and he started as an office boy with a paper and cardboard company. War was on the horizon: air raid shelters were being constructed; gas masks issued; trenches dug; iron railings melted down; and his company was asked to quote for 20,000 cardboard coffins. And then he fell in love again …

Photo – Anon

A 1938 photograph of Brenda Pool sent to Antony's mother during the war

London
August 1939

Dear Friend

I am so much in love that whenever I think of my sweetheart I find myself quoting Shakespeare...

O, when mine eyes did see Brenda first,
Methought she purg'd the air of pestilence!
That instant was I turn'd into a hart;
And my desires, like fell and cruel hounds,
E'er since pursue me.

You see...Twelfth Night!

Brenda is beautiful, sophisticated and urbane, not to mention that her father is very rich. We are classmates at Labour Stage and after the theatre last week she took me to her home. Her parents were upstairs asleep and I felt like Romeo sneaking into the Capulet house to deflower Juliet. What would her father do if he heard noises? Would he take me as a burglar? Did he have a shotgun? The stage was set with subdued lighting and soft carpets, but I wilted at the thought of being caught and Brenda tried to stiffen me up with a few drinks from her father's cabinet. Now I worried he would kill me for stealing his booze. She did her best but nothing worked.

It was after 2am when we kissed goodnight on Brenda's doorstep and it was a scene straight out of Romeo and Juliet...

Good night, good night! parting is such sweet sorrow
Then I shall say good night till it be morrow.

But I was heady from the drink and Brenda's sweet perfume and missed the bus. So I walked... all night, thinking only of what might have been So near, yet so far. In the end I walked all the way home and found my dinner left from the previous night – cold tinned herrings. I fear that I will never be able to face a cold herring again.

War is coming. My landlord is polishing the bullets he kept from the last war and he's eager to slaughter Jerries again. But I don't want to fight anyone. I'm too young to die, and still a virgin. I am reminded of Shakespeare's Henry V...

Now all the youth of England are on fire,
And silken dalliance in the wardrobe lies:
Now thrive the armourers, and honour's thought
Reigns solely in the breast of every man:

Antony

In April 1939 conscription was introduced in Britain and all able-bodied men aged twenty were called up for military service. Antony was only nineteen at the time, but he could read the writing on the wall. The Nazis and Fascists were gaining ground across Europe and ill treatment of Jews in German held territory caused an exodus. Antony was asked by a friend to go through a marriage of convenience to a Jewish/ German girl so that she could obtain residence in England. He didn't comprehend the horror of what was happening at the time and declined. In any case, he still had his sights firmly set on Brenda Pool.

And then, on Sunday, September 3, 1939, he had arranged to meet Brenda at 11am for a picnic on Primrose Hill near her home in Hampstead. She wasn't at the meeting place when he arrived and a note pinned to a tree said she had gone home to hear the Prime Minister, Neville Chamberlain, speak on the radio. As Antony was reading the note the air raid sirens signaled the start of World War II.

Germany wasn't Britain's only foe at this time and Antony's first wartime experience was an IRA bomb that blasted a nearby power station and blew out all the windows at Labour Stage. The school soldiered on for a few months, but with most of the students being called up for military service it eventually closed its doors. Antony was, and always had been, an actor and wanted nothing to do with war, nevertheless, despite his pacifist beliefs, he realized that Hitler and Mussolini had to be stopped and so he attended the army recruiting office when called. The British army has always had a reputation (sometimes deserved) for placing men in unsuitable positions, but when Antony said he was an actor the recruiter sensed that he would be good at communications and enlisted him in The Royal Corps of Signals

Nelson Illingworth wrote of Antony at that time that he had a marked talent for acting, adding, "This will without doubt ultimately lead him to genuine success on the stage". However, the war not only put paid to any immediate hope of theatrical stardom for Antony, but his return home to Tiverton to await his call-up papers also ruined his chances of ever hitting the jackpot in Brenda Pool's bedroom.

Antony was at a loose end while he waited in Devon and was itching to get back on the stage, so he assembled some past members of the Tiverton School of Art Dramatic Society and formed The Tiverton Dramatic Society*, carefully avoiding the term 'amateur'. His modus

---

* In 2010 the Tiverton Dramatic Society, founded by Antony, celebrated its 70th anniversary.

24

operandi was to form a theatrical group and then direct them in a play in which he took the lead. It was a process that he repeated successfully many times over the next few years.

Antony's first full length play with the dramatic society was *Night Must Fall* by Emlyn Williams and, of course, he cast himself in the key role of the charming psychopathic murderer named Danny. To practice the Welsh accent for his role, Antony took a Welshman to a pub on three consecutive nights and bought him beers – not a hard thing to do – but he still needed a leading lady for the part of the ingénue, Olivia Grayne.

Dorothy Colebrook, now in her nineties, vividly recalls the day in 1940 when she was doling out fuel ration coupons in a Tiverton office and Antony spotted her. She was a young, vivacious, twenty two year old, so shouldn't have been too surprised when Antony waited till she was alone in the office to proposition her. But Antony had only one thing on his mind. "Would you like to be in a play?" he said, and she was taken completely off-guard.

"I would never have thought of it if he hadn't asked," she admits, adding, "He said he liked my voice, and he could be very persuasive. He pushed me into it, but I didn't realize I was being manipulated. He never asked me for a date – he was only interested in the theatre and our performance."

Dorothy still has a strong clear voice with a touch of class as she recounts how Antony taught her to act and to fall. "Antony took the play very seriously," she says, "We had good audiences and old-timers in Tiverton still talk about the performance today, seventy years later."

Involvement in The Tiverton Dramatic Society changed Dorothy's future. She met her husband on the stage and stayed involved in drama all her life, thanks entirely, she says, to Antony.

The three performances at Heathcoat Hall in Tiverton at the end of April 1940 only covered expenses, but the Tiverton Dramatic Society was born. *Night Must Fall* was reprised on May 7 of that year, in aid of The Red Cross, and again in the Drill Hall in Uffculme on Thursday, May 9. The numerous reviews were all in accord: The play, the production, the direction and the acting were all outstanding. "Mr. Holland gave a brilliant portrayal as Dan", gushed one reviewer while another pointed out that, "Mr. A.E.Holland is the driving force behind the society".

However, Antony's fledgling career was shot down by the arrival of his call-up papers. But he wouldn't go to war without a swansong and on June 14 he presented his own farewell performance of *Night Must Fall*, casting many of the same players who had appeared in The Tiverton Dramatic Society's performances. This time he appointed himself sole producer and director, and even took two parts, and then pronounced that this would be his final performance with as much fanfare as if he was retiring after a lifetime on the stage.

Act 3

And So To War...

Then a soldier,
Full of strange oaths and bearded like the pard,
Jealous in honour, sudden and quick in quarrel,
Seeking the bubble reputation
Even in the cannon's mouth.

(Shak. As You Like It)

Somewhere in Wales
August 1940

Dear Mum and Dad

     I'm in the army now, although I'm not allowed to tell you exactly where in case Hitler finds out. (I bet you had no idea your son was so important to the war effort!). I'll give you a clue – I'm at the seaside and there's a big sign saying "Welcome to Butlin's Holiday Camp" across the front gates of the camp.

I'm having lots of fun running around with a huge pack on my back, shooting at things, going to the beach and getting lots of good food. (My corporal said I had to write all this nice stuff because our letters are censored),

Anyway, I'm still alive, I think, and I've already been in trouble for saluting a sergeant major, for not making my bed properly and having my hair too long.

Can you believe that our regimental march is, "Begone dull care, I Prithee begone from me." Whoever chose it must have been on the same course as me.

Antony

The army camp in Llandudno, North Wales, where Signalman 2347625 A.E.Holland attended basic infantry training had never been a Butlin's holiday camp. Some wag had put the sign over the entrance as a joke but Antony didn't know that. In fact, he never knew he had been fooled by the sign until seventy years later. But a grueling six week course of parades, gymnastics, rifle drills, forced marches in full kit, and hours of spit and polish, was certainly no holiday for Antony. However, he beat the system somewhat when he discovered a short cut that circumnavigated a particularly steep and difficult hill that he was supposed to climb with a heavy pack, and, contrary to regulations, he padded his shoulder before every rifle practice to reduce the pain of recoils.

Other than when Antony and his fellow greenhorns were slogging around the countryside on punishing route marches, they were confined to barracks for the entire six weeks, unlike their dirty clothes which were sent out to a local laundry. One day Antony's clothes returned with a young laundress' name and address suggestively attached. Had she fallen in love with him based solely on his underwear? He often wondered, but never found out.

Antony's youngest brother, Kaye, recalls the day Antony arrived home after joining the army and says, "If ever we were worried that Hitler might win the war – it was that day. There was a knock on the side door of the milk bar and when I opened it there stood my brother, wearing a uniform that would have fitted someone twice his size, carrying a long-barreled Lee Enfield rifle by his side. The British Army had almost turned my brother into a man."

Following his basic training in Llandudno, Signalman Holland traveled by train to London carrying his full kit and uniform – something he was required to do in case he was suddenly called to duty. When he arrived on September 7 he telephoned Ruby, an ex-student at Labour Stage, to arrange a meeting. She had become a nurse and agreed to meet later that evening but only if there was no air raid. So Antony booked in to the YMCA to await his date and was sitting on the toilet when, without warning, a huge explosion shook the building and sent him crashing headfirst into the toilet door. Explosions continued as he picked himself off the floor and, despite his muzzy-headedness, he realized that he had to get to a shelter immediately. Many buildings were on fire as he ran down the street with bombs and debris falling all around him. He was disorientated by the blast, but an air raid warden grabbed him and sent him down the tube station in Trafalgar Square. When he surfaced from the shelter, following the 'all-clear' many hours later, it seemed that the whole city was on fire. German incendiaries had ignited large areas of London; entire streets were in flames. The iconic dome of St.Paul's Cathedral was ringed by an inferno that illuminated it against the sky. It was the most damaging attack on London of the entire Blitz, yet both St.Paul's Cathedral and Signalman A.E.Holland survived. However, he never did get his date with Ruby.

With his leave over, Antony was transferred to a former school in South Shields in the North of England to learn Morse code so that he could become a wireless operator, but in late 1940 he became homesick – not for his home in far off Devon – for the stage. With a little research he discovered that a well equipped local theatre was dark because the war had killed off many of the touring companies that normally appeared there and, in no time at all, he persuaded his corporal to become his business manager, got financial backing from a local wealthy widow, put together a group of local amateurs with some of his fellow signalmen, and formed the Royal Signals' Dramatic Society. Their first production was, perhaps unsurprisingly, *Night Must Fall,* and it was held in aid of a Royal Signals' charity fund. Antony, of course, took the leading role of Danny, and then annoyed his fellow students at the school by practicing his lines in Morse code during lessons. While his colleagues may not have appreciated having to decipher the complex language of the play, the show's audience and the local newspaper's theatre critic certainly did, and it was a great success.

Following Britain's hurried retreat from Dunkirk in the spring of 1940 the allied forces only ground offensive was in North Africa, defending Egypt from the Italians amassed in Libya, and after spending a pleasant Christmas with a family in South Shields at the end of his course Antony received orders to sail for Cairo where he was to deploy as a tank radio operator.

Any soldier sent to the front in the 1940s had no expectation of seeing his family again before the end of war – if ever, so it was customary for men to receive a few weeks leave to spend with their folks prior to embarkation. And so, after being given an armful of inoculations against tropical diseases, Antony set off home by train, via London, lugging with him all his kit and his rifle. He didn't get far before feeling

Photo — Anon

Antony as 'Dan' and Winifred Crawford as 'Olivia' in the 1940 production
of *Night Must Fall* in South Shields, (December 8, 1940)

ill and by the time he got to St. Pancras in London he was so faint that he had to be helped off the train by a military policeman and given a bed in a hut, just outside the station, which was reserved for soldiers in transit. He was told an ambulance would be sent in the morning if he was no better. There was a major air raid on London that night and bombs fell all round St. Pancras and the neighbouring station at King's Cross. The noise of exploding bombs and the answering bursts of anti-aircraft guns would have been deafening inside Antony's flimsy lodging, but he was hallucinating with fever and thought it was probably a nightmare. So he just stayed in the hut and waited till the morning when the ambulance crew found him – surrounded by ruins and broken glass. However, both he and his hut were completely unscathed in the attack.

After a few weeks in hospital with an undiagnosed fever Antony learned that his deployment to Africa had been delayed, and he was given three weeks sick leave in recompense for his lost time before being ordered to report to a transit camp in a commandeered country house in Bakewell, Derbyshire.

Bakewell is a market town in the Peak District, a highland area in the hinterland of England renowned for its wicked winter weather, and the building that housed the troops was a draughty old manor with no heating other than a small fireplace in each room. Antony and his colleagues spent much of their time scavenging wood and coal from the surrounding areas in order to keep the fires burning while they waited for their ship to Egypt, but otherwise they had little to do.

In order to relieve the boredom, Antony began looking for a way to get back on the stage and discovered that the town had an amateur theatrical group, known as The Peacock Players, which performed on a small stage in the town hall. By now Antony had cast himself as a fully fledged professional actor/director with a string of credits from London, Tiverton and South Shields, so it didn't take him long to convince the locals that they should present *Night Must Fall* with him in the lead role.

With the assistance of some of his fellow servicemen, and with the backing of his regiment, Antony produced yet another acclaimed performance of Emlyn Williams' play in aid of the Royal Corps of Signals' charity. And one of the women involved in the production, a Miss Olivia Hearty-Hudson, must have fallen for Antony's charms because she continued writing to him throughout the war.

Act 4

Voyage to Africa

And you, good yeoman,
Whose limbs were made in England, show us here
The mettle of your pasture;

(Shak. Henry V)

After a year of training, while Hitler's bombers continued to blitz English city after English city, Antony and the thousands of other servicemen who boarded a fleet of converted freighters in Liverpool docks en-route to the North African front in the spring of 1941 finally felt they were doing their part to engage the enemy. But it was potentially a suicide mission. The Italians and Germans outnumbered the British and their allies – Australians, New Zealanders, South Africans and Indians – by three to one, and they could easily ship reinforcements and supplies across the Mediterranean to Libya. Whereas the British were forced to supply their army by a circuitous five to six week voyage around the South African Cape to avoid German U-Boats and land based torpedo bombers stationed in occupied Europe.

The dozen ships in the British convoy were accompanied out of the River Mersey into the Irish Sea by two Royal Navy destroyers and at first headed northwest, toward Greenland, before dropping the escort and zigzagging southwards down the centre of the Atlantic, beyond the Germans' range.

While the officers had cabins on the upper decks, Antony and his mates were crammed into the ships' holds where they slept in hammocks strung above the long dining tables. The toilets were communal, eight in a row, with no privacy whatsoever, and Antony was so inhibited he didn't go for a week. An almost lethal dose of cascara from the ship's doctor caused him yet another explosive toilet incident.

There was no room for military drills or routines aboard the overcrowded ship so the men spent their time reading, playing cards or, contrary to regulations, gambling, and it wasn't long before Antony started a drama group. With a lengthy voyage ahead of them, Antony's unit commander had suggested he should take some scripts along in order to put on some plays to keep the troops entertained. He was permitted the use of the officers' lounge for rehearsals, and volunteers showed up in droves once word leaked out that cold beer could be bought there. With days and nights free to learn lines and rehearse, the drama group presented a different play each week – all with male characters only and Antony again played Shylock in the trial scene from *The Merchant of Venice*. Costumes were simple; cloaks were made from the curtains in the officers' lounge and a crown for the Duke of Venice materialized from the padding inside a tin helmet. And all was going well when disaster struck …

Ship's Hospital
Somewhere in the South Atlantic
April 1941

Dear Friend

The only reason that you are reading this is because I've died of my wounds and you have received my personal effects.

Now, you might imagine that my ship was torpedoed by a U-boat and I was strafed by German machine gunners while heroically trying to rescue my shipmates from a burning ocean...or something along those lines. You can tell my family that if you like – but the truth is I was beaten to a pulp by a gorilla and I hurt in places where I didn't even realize I had places.

What happened?

Well some of the lads on the ship were getting a bit bored so a sadistic idiot thought we should hold boxing matches between mess tables … and I lost the toss.

"I'm just an actor," I kept telling them, and they said, "Well act like a man then and give him a good hiding. Anyway, it's only three rounds."

You should have seen the size of the brute. To make matters worse he was a southpaw with a vicious left uppercut and my so called 'trainer' had only taught me to fight right-handers.

Hoping to soothe the savage beast, I quoted Shakespeare from Henry VI, *"True nobility is exempt from fear:"* I boldly shouted, *"More can I bear than you dare execute."*

That stopped him, for a second...then he knocked me about something fierce: punches to the head; blows to the body; hooks to the chin and several fists in places I'd rather not talk about. I barely made it back to my corner after the first bell. There was blood everywhere – and it was all mine! The referee could see I was in trouble. It was obvious that I was seriously outmatched and he was so concerned about the punishment I was taking that he tossed a coin to decide whether he should stop the match or let it go the full three rounds. I lost that toss as well.

I'll write again – if I live

Antony

Antony lived and got back on his feet, though he never boxed again, and as the ship neared the Cape of Good Hope it encountered some heavy Atlantic swells that had him and his fellow actors staggering like drunks from one side of the stage to the other. In the middle of one performance the entire front row of the audience slid helplessly off the end of their bench and tumbled into a heap on the deck.

After rounding the Cape they put into the port of Durban to obtain fresh supplies and give the men shore leave. Before disembarkation Antony and his pals were warned of the dangers of fraternizing with black or coloured women and of drinking the local brandy – potentially deadly firewater. Naturally, he and the others tried the brandy. But during the voyage Antony had read Upton Sinclair's novel, *The Jungle*, in which workers who accidentally slipped into meat processing vats in Chicago had ended up in cans for the army and, because all the meat served aboard was canned, he had become a vegetarian. Now, with the warnings about the local women and alcohol ringing in his ears, he seriously considered becoming a celibate vegetarian abstainer for the rest of his tour.

The British flotilla eventually arrived at their disembarkation point in Egypt and the troops were paraded onto trains bound for Cairo. After a short spell in barracks, where he was falsely accused and convicted of harbouring bedbugs in his mattress, Antony was deployed to a Royal Corps of Signals' camp in the desert close to the village of Maadi, an upper class enclave of wealthy Egyptians and ex-pat Europeans which boasted a swimming pool, golf course and school, twenty miles south of the Egyptian capital on the banks of the Nile.

Accommodation was rudimentary in the camp. There were a few Nissan huts housing the orderly room, stores, first-aid post and mess, while the men slept in canvas tents partially sunk into the sand to keep them cool. It very rarely rains in the eastern stretches of the Sahara Desert and the shine soon wears off the constantly blazing sun when there is little shade, but bed bugs and sand fleas were the major irritant at the camp and numerous efforts were made to eradicate them. One solution was to stand the legs of the bed in small cans containing paraffin, (kerosene). This deterred the bugs from climbing up, but nothing stopped them from dropping from the canvas roof. Everybody suffered, some more than others, so each week all the bedding was left out in the blistering sun for a day in the hope that the heat would incinerate the pesky creatures.

When Antony arrived in Egypt, General Wavell, the allied Commander-in-Chief, had outwitted his adversary, Marshall Graziani, and the entire Italian Tenth Army had surrendered and had been shipped to India to sit out the war in POW camps. However, things were changing; Field Marshall Rommel had been sent with the elite Afrikakorps to push the allies out of Libya.

Fighting was taking place, but the front was nearly 500 kilometres away in Tobruk and Benghazi, so as Antony and scores of other newly minted radio operators assembled for their first early morning parade at the Maadi camp, they found themselves eagerly staring across an empty desert wondering if they would ever see a tank. The tanks were there, in the far distant Western Desert, but at that time there were only a few hundred and the military brass had grossly overestimated the number of radio operators required to man them. There was nothing for the new arrivals to do, but the military abhors idleness so volunteers were called for.

'Never volunteer' was a motto drummed into all young soldiers as it was well known that sergeant majors would con enlisted men to undertake dangerous or dirty jobs by asking for volunteers for seemingly innocuous or even pleasant tasks. For instance, 'a spot of gardening' could mean days of digging latrine trenches … 'a bit of local sightseeing' might include a dangerous foray behind enemy lines. So, when the sergeant major asked for a volunteer who could type, Antony took something of a risk. It paid off on this occasion and he ended up typing out all kinds of official correspondence in the relative safety and comfort of the camp's orderly room.

Many old soldiers tell hair-raising tales of a bible or a silver cigarette case in their breast pocket stopping a bullet, but few can honestly claim that their lives were saved by an ancient Olivetti typewriter. Antony Holland is one who makes that claim. The old manual typewriter assigned to him by the orderly room sergeant was a museum piece, but he eventually mastered it, became invaluable as the company's clerk and, as a result, never got to the frontlines and never saw action as a radio operator in a tank.

Daily life in the camp was routine and, following breakfast and early morning inspection, Antony spent his days in the office typing military orders and lists of supplies on the cumbersome machine. His evenings were free and the bars and movie theatres of Cairo were only thirty minutes away by train. However, Cairo had something else to offer that many of Antony's cohorts found quite irresistible – whorehouses. While the Islamic Egyptian authorities may have frowned on the establishments, the allied military had been more pragmatic and set up medical facilities outside the major brothels to provide advice and prophylactics to curb the spread of sexually transmitted diseases.

Under pressure from his colleagues, Antony finally succumbed to his carnal desires …

Cairo
June 1941

Dear Friend

Shakespeare! – Sometimes I think he knows me better than I know myself.

"I know that a woman is a dish for the gods, if the devil dress her not." the Bard wrote, but what was I supposed to do? Twenty one, and the furthest south I'd ever got with a woman was the elastic waistband of Brenda Pool's undies. *"Keep thy foot out of brothels, thy hand out of plackets,"* Edgar says in Lear, but it was all right for him, he wasn't surrounded by hundreds of horny squaddies stuck in the Egyptian desert waiting to go to the front. What if I should die a virgin? So I went to a brothel in Cairo last night with some of the lads.

I had a drink – a couple actually – and I was nervously excited when I pushed open the door and saw her lying, nearly naked, on the bed in the glow of a red lamp...an Egyptian princess. "Come inside, handsome," she said in a husky voice and I knew exactly what she meant, so I straightened myself against the doorpost, raised my right fist triumphantly in the air and gave her those immortal lines from Antony and Cleopatra: *"Antony shall be brought drunken forth, and I shall see some squeaking Cleopatra boy my greatness I' the posture of a whore."*

I could tell she wasn't used to Shakespeare by the look on her face. "Have you been drinking?" she said, and I lied, but half an hour later I realized that I had used the wrong speech. I should have quoted from Macbeth. You know, the part when MacDuff asks, *"What three things does drink especially provoke?"* and Porter replies: *"Lechery, sir, it provokes, and unprovokes; it provokes the desire, but it takes away the performance."*

Antony
(Still virgo intacto!)

Antony insists that his failure to launch into manhood may have had more to do with his fear of catching a venereal disease than his consumption of Dutch courage, but his anxiety over his virginity was not his greatest concern. He wanted to get back on the stage and had approached a number of Europeans connected to amateur groups in Cairo with an eye to producing and directing a play. He made several attempts but, as a lowly army private, he was totally out of his depth with Cairo's snobbish ex-pat colonials and was given the cold shoulder. He was also rebuffed by the NAAFI* and several other official agencies charged with entertaining the troops and, finally, by his own regimental welfare officer who scoffed at the idea of a mere signalman putting on a play, despite the fact that Antony provided his acting credentials along with a tattered scrapbook of reviews and photos from his earlier performances.

However, love will always find a way, and Antony's luck changed when he was charged with failing to lay out his equipment in accordance with regulations and not cleaning his rifle properly. He received a reprimand, but two of his tent mates were punished by being transferred out and replaced by two corporals-of-the-horse. (NCOs of a cavalry regiment whose horses had actually been replaced with tanks but had kept their titles because of tradition, and because "Corporal-of-the-tank" sounded silly).

One of the corporals, David Okely, had been present when the welfare officer had mocked Antony's request to stage a play. "I was not fearfully impressed myself", he later wrote to his parents, but as he got to know Antony he became more interested and agreed to help in any way possible.

Corporal Okely, now co-opted by Antony as his business and publicity manager, knew of a large recreation tent in the nearby village of Maadi where European civilians provided coffee, tea and homemade sandwiches to the troops, and Antony was back in love – not with a woman, but with a large unused stage at one end of the tent. Antony immediately called the stage his own and set about putting on yet another production of *Night Must Fall*. He roped in the other corporal, Don Dansi, to stage manage, and quickly recruited the male cast, both from his own camp and from a nearby New Zealanders' camp. He

*NAAFI – Navy, Army and Air Force Institutes. (Provides recreational, leisure and shopping services to U.K. servicemen worldwide).

needed five women to make up the ensemble and persuaded four of the tent's civilian helpers to participate, together with a young ATS* girl, Kay Davies.

Antony soon amassed a backstage crew of about twenty to provide costumes, scenery, lighting and general support, and began rehearsals in a local school. And then he really fell in love…Laila was a twenty-something Anglo-Egyptian with a Scottish mother, whose father was the Egyptian Minister of Agriculture. She only had a minor role in the play because Antony hadn't been impressed with her acting during auditions. However, the attractive young woman had a number of assets that certainly impressed Antony, including her father's flashy American car in which they would canoodle after rehearsals when she drove him back to his camp. But Antony's hormone war was raging. He had suffered defeat after defeat in his attempts at consummation and a little innocent canoodling wasn't enough: he wanted nirvana. Laila was both patient and understanding and explained matter-of-factly that in a few months she would be marrying another man and that as soon as the wedding had taken place she would be free to give Antony everything he craved. And so, in time, yet another of Antony's unrequited romantic adventures bit the dust.

Rehearsals lasted several weeks. Antony took no chances when it came to working with inexperienced amateurs. He insisted that they were 'off-book' early in the process and he relentlessly drilled them in the techniques of stagecraft until he was completely satisfied with their performance.

David Okely, as promoter and business manager, had done an excellent job in publicizing the play; getting articles in two of the major English language newspapers in addition to a number of military journals. Consequently, there was a great deal of interest in the show. Two performances had been scheduled originally but demand for tickets was so great that a third night was added. Close to two thousand soldiers and civilians attended and the shows were a terrific success.

Two respected war correspondents attended the opening night performance: James Lonsdale Hodson of The Egyptian Mail and William Forrest of the British News Chronicle. They both gave the show glowing reviews and Hodson later wrote in his war memoirs, titled *War in the Sun*:

* Auxiliary Territorial Service. (U.K.)

"Danny was played by a signaler of twenty one, who toured in the part in Britain – he gave a first-rate, mature and confident portrayal of the Welsh murderer-exhibitionist".

A successful short run in the entertainment tent in Maadi was certainly a major coup for Antony, especially as he had previously been shunned by both the civilian and military establishment, but neither he nor his team of amateurs could possibly have imagined that they would soon be performing to sold out audiences in one of the most prestigious theatres in the world.

Act 5

Success on the Nile

A very riband in the cap of youth.

(Shak. Hamlet)

Photo - Anon

The stage of The Royal Opera House, Cairo.
Set for Antony's production of *Night Must Fall,* (December 18, 1941)

The Royal Opera House
Cairo
December 18,1941

Dear Mum

I told you I would be famous one day. Your son, Signalman A.E.Holland has his name in lights in Cairo. Can you believe it? But not just Cairo... The Royal Opera House, Cairo – one of the most splendid theatres in the world. It was opened in 1869 to celebrate the Suez Canal and some of the most famous actors and singers in the world have performed here. Verdi himself stood on this stage in 1871 for the world premiere of Aida.

And now, my name has been added to list. 'Antony Holland ... Producer, Director and Star of Emlyn Williams' *Night Must Fall.* I even got a 'Good Luck' telegram from Williams himself.

It was a full house last night; nearly a thousand people all clapping and cheering, and then, and I can still hardly believe this myself, the stage manager rushed into the dressing room and said that Sir Miles Lampson, the British Ambassador, wanted to meet the cast. We all dashed back onstage after the second curtain and stood in line while the Ambassador and his wife went along shaking hands, thanking us and saying really nice things about the show, and then a stranger in evening dress came out of the wings and walked across the stage. "I expect you know each other," said Sir Miles with a grin, "You're in the same outfit." I thought Sir Miles meant that the guy was in the Signal Corps – probably some big-shot sent from HQ to make sure we didn't embarrass the regiment – so I nearly fell over when he shook my hand and told me that he was <u>God</u> himself. Yes, Mum, it was Lieutenant General, Sir Claude Auchinleck – none other than the Commander-in-Chief of allied forces in the Middle East.

Must dash – Three more shows to do and all sold out!

It was, as Osric says in Hamlet, "*A hit, a very palpable hit.*"

Your Son

Antony

Antony's meteoric rise to fame from the recreation tent in Maadi to the splendour of Cairo's grand Royal Opera House began on the second night of the show in Maadi, when a sergeant from the army's welfare office at Abbassia Barracks in Cairo arrived with a request from a captain in the Royal Engineers, Jasper Maskelyne.

Captain Maskelyne had been an eminent professional magician in pre-war Britain who had stunned his audiences with incredible illusions. He joined the Royal Engineers at the outbreak of war and, by using mirrors and a scale model to create the image of a German warship sailing up the Thames into London, convinced skeptical commanders that subterfuge could be an important component of modern warfare.

In January 1941 General Wavell had created the 'A Force' in North Africa and recruited Captain Maskelyne to lead a team of artists, engineers, painters and set designers to outwit the enemy. 'The Magic Gang', as they were known, built a dummy harbour and replicated the strategic port of Alexandria in a nearby, uninhabited, bay to bamboozle Luftwaffe bomb aimers, and they made the Suez Canal invisible to enemy pilots with a complex system of searchlights and spinning mirrors. Maskelyne was also the inventor of camouflage netting, and he was instrumental in the final defeat of the Germans at El Alamein when he disguised 1,000 tanks as trucks in the north, and created 2,000 mock tanks out of plywood in the southern desert. He even built false railway lines and a fake pipeline, and created bogus communications and phony construction noise to fool the Germans.

Early on in the campaign in North Africa, Maskelyne and his team had time on their hands and built a large theatre in Cairo, called the Garrison Opera House. He wanted an opening night performance at his new theatre which would draw in crowds of servicemen and, after hearing of Antony's success in Maadi, decided on *Night Must Fall*. Antony was reluctant to agree when first asked because the theatre was still under construction, but in the end everything went to plan and there were two sold out performances.

With successes at Maadi, and Maskelyne's Garrison Opera House in Cairo, Antony and his troupe were on a roll and thought they should take the show on the road, or across the desert, to other camps. Transportation was the issue. Antony's unit commander had provided transport to Maskelyne's theatre for the set and the cast (and the civilian women had thought it great fun to ride in the back of an army truck), but to tour on a wider scale would require official authorization and Antony was directed to apply to a major in Cairo who was in charge of providing entertainment for the troops.

A meeting was arranged and while Antony's right hand men, Corporals Okely and Dansi, nervously waited in the street outside the major's office, he stood to attention inside and delivered his request. But he got the cold shoulder. "Troops aren't interested in plays", claimed the officer, without even standing Antony at ease. "All they want is musicals and girls with big tits". Antony had hardly opened his mouth to ask permission to speak when the major shouted, "Dismiss", and he found himself back on the pavement with his mates.

That was it, the show was over, and Antony and his team drowned their sorrows in a bar before heading for the railway station and their desert home in Maadi. Their route to the station took them through Meidan el Opera Square, past Cairo's opulent Royal Opera House, and David Okely drunkenly suggested that that was where they should put the play on – and not go begging for a truck to take them around army camps in the desert. The others laughed at his stupidity.

But the show wasn't over. Lady Jacqueline Lampson, the wife of Sir Miles Lampson, the British Ambassador in Egypt, was raising money to provide Christmas gifts to all the wounded British troops in hospital that year, and she had formed a committee of her peers to help. Having heard about Antony's remarkable success with *Night Must Fall* she sent an emissary to David Okely to ask if the show could be reprised as a fundraiser for her charitable cause.

Okely, now with some very high powered backing, decided that the Royal Opera House was not so stupid after all, especially as the theatre was barely used because the touring Italian opera companies that normally appeared there were no longer welcome.

Suliman Bey Nequib, the Opera House manager, was a tall aristocratic Egyptian accustomed to wearing European clothes topped by a bright red fez, and when he met Antony a few days later he showed a great knowledge and love of English theatre, even enquiring after Gielgud and Olivier. Antony was itching to know whether or not he could produce a play at the Opera House, but Nequib was in no hurry to put him out of his misery and entered into a lengthy discussion about theatre in general. In the end Antony could stand the strain no longer and asked if it would be possible. "Oh yes. I would very much like to have it in my Opera House", the manager replied, as if it was already a done deal, but when Antony asked the cost he was stopped by an outstretched hand. "We are artists", said Nequib, "We do not discuss money. I will send you the contract".

The contract was generous. There were no rental or scenery construction fees, and the backstage staff of the Opera House would all be at Antony's disposal. In return the Opera House would take 40% of the box-office, leaving Lady Lampson's Christmas Stocking Gift Scheme 60% after expenses.

Producing a high profile stage show in a world class theatre might be beyond the capabilities of many twenty one year olds, but Antony took it all in his stride. He was the only 'professional' in the team, and certainly had as much formal training as Gielgud and many of the other young actor/managers of the day. Antony was also the same age as Shakespeare had been when he found success as an actor, and part owner, of a London company of players in 1585.

The Royal Opera House in Cairo was a magnificent wooden building with spectacular architecture, lavish furnishings and sumptuous features. It had been designed by Italian architects Avoscani and Rossi to provide a dramatic venue for classical opera. The enormous proscenium stage, with plush red curtains, looked out onto a horseshoe shaped auditorium with many tiers of gorgeously decorated boxes and circles. Until it accidentally burned to the ground in the early hours of October 28, 1971, Cairo's Royal Opera House was recognized as one of the most beautiful theatres in the world.

In 1941 the theatre had more than 2,000 sets of scenery, props and costumes from seventy years' productions, and Shukri, the stage manager, was able to provide Antony with a magnificent set for the show. Lighting, however, was more problematic. The chief electrician was a partially deaf Italian, and he headed a team of six Egyptians on a high platform at the back of the stage. It was an antiquated lighting system operated by huge wheels that required much effort and shouting by all involved. Fortunately, Antony's lighting plot was fairly simple, but it had to be in both Arabic and Italian and was eventually accomplished with lots of hand signals and the aid of an interpreter.

The set requested by Antony didn't exactly resemble the living room of a cozy English cottage because of the size of the stage. The fifteen foot wide bay window, centre back, was clearly out of place, but Antony decided that he would live with it. Conversely, the enormous chandelier hanging at centre stage would have to go. Shukri agreed. However, on the second night of rehearsals the chandelier had simply been replaced by a different one. When Antony complained, the stage manager shiftily explained that as most operas had several chandeliers there were two men on staff, one to let down a rope and another to hook the chandelier on, and that these men had very large families. Antony took the hint and realized that the only way he could lose the chandelier was to pay the men to do nothing.

Corporal David Okely was again in charge of publicity and the box-office, and he did an amazing job of procuring and distributing several thousand posters. The cause was worthy so the press were very helpful in promoting the show, but there were a couple of last minute hitches. The show was advertised to run for just three nights in mid December, but ten days before the opening night the city authorities announced that Cairo would be blacked out on two of them. Neither the Germans nor the Italians had bombed Cairo up to that point and it was speculated that the Axis powers were hoping to take Egypt without destroying the city and upsetting the natives. Nonetheless, the Egyptians were taking no chances and planned to test their blackout precautions.

There was much debate within Antony's troupe as to the potential effect of a blackout, so an afternoon matinee was added to the program to cater to anyone who was reluctant to attend at night. As it turned out the blackouts didn't adversely affect the box-office at all, and may even have encouraged people to attend in order to avoid sitting in their darkened houses.

The second hitch involved the Lord Chief Justice's wig which, for some reason, the Opera House wardrobe department was unable to supply. The wardrobe master and Antony's stage manager, Don Dansi, were sent to scour Cairo for a suitable hairpiece, but two hours later returned with empty hands and empty pockets. They had been unable to buy a wig, so had blown the money they were given in a bar.

December 17, 1941 was the opening night, and Antony could hardly believe his eyes when he sneaked to the front of the Opera House and watched Cairo's civilian elite, together with senior military officers and diplomats, arriving in limousines. The officers were all wearing full dress uniforms while their wives and many civilians were in formal evening wear.

With just five minutes to curtain call, stage manager Shukri surprised Antony by saying that the British Embassy had called to say that Ambassador Lampson would be a few minutes late but that they shouldn't hold the curtain. It had not occurred to Antony that the Ambassador himself would attend, despite the fact that his wife was the patron of the Christmas stocking fund. As it happened, the Ambassador arrived just as the curtain rose and the show started smoothly. The audience was enthralled throughout the first act, and Antony was just getting ready for Act 2 when he was informed that Sir Miles wished to meet the entire cast during the second intermission.

Antony and the rest of the cast were suitably impressed when Suliman Bey Nequib, the general manager, introduced Lord Lampson and Jacqueline, his diminutive young Italian wife. "Jolly good show young man", said the Ambassador, and then he dropped a bombshell by bringing in the allied forces Commander-in-Chief, Sir Claude Auchinleck. Antony kept his cool as Auchinleck, his ultimate boss, praised the performance, adding, "It's a pity we couldn't take this to some of the camps".

"We wanted to, Sir", replied Antony, "But we had difficulty getting transport".

"Really!" said the C-in-C, "Come and see me in my office at GHQ tomorrow morning at 10 o'clock".

David Okely wrote to his mother after the show and said that Antony went back onstage and played the final act like he had never played it before. "He rose to the occasion like a hero", wrote Okely, before adding that the show was a tremendous success and the press write-ups were so magnificent that they could have sold out ten more shows if the Opera House had been available.

Act 6

The Theatre of War

And all the gods go with you! Upon your sword
Sit laurel victory! And smooth success
Be strew'd before your feet!

(Shak. Antony & Cleopatra)

Thunderous applause was still ringing in Antony's ears the following morning when he reported to a skeptical military policeman guarding the Commander-in-Chief's headquarters. The redcap clearly didn't believe that a lowly signalman had an appointment with the top man, leaving Antony to wonder if Auchinleck had simply been polite in front of the Ambassador and never really expected a mere 'grunt' to have the nerve to beard him in his lair. Nevertheless, the gates opened and a few minutes later Antony was sitting outside Auchinleck's office when the lieutenant general strolled along the corridor. Antony sprang to attention and saluted, but the general disappeared into his office and shut the door without a word. That sealed it for Antony; he had obviously misread Auchinleck's invitation and was thinking of slinking quietly away when the commanding officer snatched open his door, saying, "I'm terribly sorry. I didn't recognize you in uniform".

The meeting that followed was extraordinary, and possibly unique in the annals of the British military, in that Antony, one of the lowest ranking soldiers in the British Army, sat chatting to a knighted lieutenant general – even smoking one of Auchinleck's cigarettes – in the privacy of the supreme commander's inner sanctum. And the upshot was that Auchinleck had been so impressed with Antony's presentation that he was to be allowed to tour his show to camps across the entire Middle East theatre of operations: Egypt; The Canal Zone; Sinai and Palestine. "We might even get you into Tobruk", Auchinleck mused excitedly, even though Tobruk had been besieged by Rommel's Afrikakorps for most of the year.

Only one detail remained, and that was a question of military protocol. "What rank are you?" enquired Auchinleck, and when Antony replied that he was just a signalman, the same as a private soldier, the general asked him what was the highest rank of anyone in his company. When Antony said that two of his team were corporals-of-the-horse, Auchinleck responded by immediately promoting him to acting sergeant so that he would have authority over them. Not that he needed it: no one in his troupe ever doubted that Antony was in charge.

With the decision made, General Auchinleck picked up his phone and ordered a planning conference of senior officers to take place that afternoon, with Antony in attendance. He then wished Antony good luck, shook his hand, and passed him on to a brigadier with instructions to take him to lunch and to make sure that he got whatever he asked for at the conference …

Photo - Angelo

Antony with Kay Davies as 'Danny and Olivia' in *Night Must Fall* (1942)

Cairo
December 19, 1941

Dear Friend

Events are moving so fast I hardly know where to begin. As Fabian said in Twelfth Night, *"If this were played upon a stage now, I could condemn it as an improbable fiction."* Last night I got a standing ovation at the Royal Opera House in Cairo, and this morning I sat down with the Commander-in-Chief and he promoted me to sergeant. In retrospect I think I undershot; when he asked me the highest rank in my crew I should have said "lieutenant" then he might have made me a captain.

Hum! ha! Is this a vision? Is this a dream?

This afternoon I sat at the head of a long table of military brass and at the far end was the major in charge of entertainments. He was the one who told me that the troops only wanted music and women with big tits. You should have seen the look on his face every time I asked for something and the brigadier said, "Can you arrange that, Major?" It wasn't a request, and the major knew it. I got everything: portable stage; lighting; scenery – even a truck and a proper bus for the cast and crew.

The best bit is that we're going to tour under the auspices of the NAAFI – and they had already turned me down! Even better – David tells me that a stuffed shirt called Bullen, one of the hoity-toity ex-pat civvies who runs the Cairo Amateur Dramatic & Musical Society, saw the first night reviews in today's papers and had to beg at the box office just to get four seats for tomorrow night's show at the Opera House. He was another of the snobs who said that respected dramatic organizations like his didn't have room for people like me. Hah! *The nonpareil of this. O, vengeance, vengeance!*

I have no time to explain everything – just three more shows at the Opera House, and then as Pistol says in The Merry Wives of Windsor: *"Why, then the world's mine oyster."*

Antony

51

Preparations for the month-long tour began as soon as the Royal Opera House run concluded. Antony and the rest of the military personnel needed consent from their individual commanders to be released from normal duties – after all, there was a war going on and they could be called to the front at any time – but all it took was a personal request from the desk of the Commander-in-Chief. All but two of the female civilians were willing to go on the tour, and they were easily replaced, although Laila's family, being Muslim, had some concerns about her being onstage: they may also have had some concerns about her being with Antony!

Antony's erstwhile nemesis, the major in the entertainment's department, arranged for a NAAFI sergeant, Noel Howlett, to act as a liaison to make sure that everything ran smoothly. Howlett had been a professional actor pre-war, appearing in London's West End, and he was given the role of supervising the construction of the portable stage, acquiring suitable transport and organizing accommodation for the troupe. The lodging arrangements caused some discontent because, while the women stayed in hotels, the men had to sleep on the ground in army transit camps. Howlett was unable to change these rules, nevertheless he became an invaluable part of the team and even broadcast a teaser on the Forces Network featuring Antony and Kay Davies, the ATS cast member, who had married just days before the tour and was on her honeymoon with her husband while on the road. Noel Howlett achieved considerable success after the war both as a movie actor and on British television.

The tour began on January 18, 1942, and received a warm reception everywhere from Jerusalem to Alexandria. However, one problem arose: at each camp the actresses were usually invited to either the officers' or sergeants' mess after the show but, as only Antony and Noel were sergeants, the other crew members were always excluded. Antony solved the problem by telling the women to refuse all invitations unless the rules were bent – so the rules were bent.

Although most performances went smoothly, a bunch of rowdy Australians in one camp decided that they preferred to prop up the bar at one end of the recreation tent rather than watch Antony and his cast performing at the other. The more intoxicated they became, the more noise they made. In the end they were shouting and laughing so much that only the first few rows of the audience could hear the play. All the other audiences were both attentive and appreciative; especially a company of Polish soldiers at a camp in Palestine. Due to lack of electrical power the stage was lit with noisy hurricane lamps that almost completely drowned out the dialogue. It didn't seem to matter – few of the Poles understood English, but, unlike the Australians, they listened politely and applauded vigorously at the end.

Antony Holland's 1942 Middle-Eastern tour of *Night Must Fall* covered two thousand miles, playing thirty three performances to audiences totaling well in excess of twenty five thousand service personnel. However, they never did get to Tobruk. Although the siege of the Libyan port had been lifted at the end of December the army brass thought it was too risky to take civilian women into a city that was still under enemy attack.

Photo – Anon

The 1942 Mid-East tour bus with cast and crew.
Antony is 2nd from left with Cpl. Don Dansi in a flat cap behind him. Kay Davies is 5th from left, (next to her husband of a few days), while Laila is the tall dark-haired girl in a white blouse to the right of the picture. Cpl. David Okely, in flat cap, is standing to right of Laila while Noel Howlett is behind her to the left.

While Antony was having a great time acting his way around Egypt and the Middle East in the early months of 1942, war had been raging on all fronts. The Japanese had attacked Pearl Harbour in December and were advancing on Burma and the Malay Peninsula, forcing the withdrawal of some British units from North Africa in order to reinforce Singapore and India. Rommel's Afrikakorps had taken the Libyan port city of Benghazi and was quickly re-supplying for a major offensive against Egypt, and the Luftwaffe was continuing to level English cities. The war was not going well for Britain and its allies.

However, the conduct of the war was of little interest to ex-Sergeant Holland, now once again a lowly signalman, back behind his desk in Maadi. Almost from the day he had received his call-up papers Antony had managed to turn military service into a means of advancing his acting career and, in a little over a year, he had formed five different acting companies (including The Tiverton Dramatic Society while awaiting basic training), and had performed his signature role of Danny in *Night Must Fall* to nearly forty thousand theatergoers. But now, as he sat at his old Olivetti in the orderly room of the Royal Signal's camp, he was preparing for an entirely new role – that of a counterespionage agent for MI5.

Photo — Angelo

Portrait of Antony by the famous Armenian photographer, Angelo.
Taken in Cairo – 1941

Photo - Angelo

Antony as Danny in *Night Must Fall* by Angelo.
Cairo – 1941

Note: This photograph and others featuring Antony as 'Danny' are held in the archives of Cairo University and have been incorrectly attributed to Angelo's equally famous brother, Van Leo.

In 2000, Fatma Bassiouni wrote a 'special' about Van Leo in the *Mideast Times*, saying, "The Van Leo photo *(sic)* of Antony Holland, a British actor stationed (in Cairo) at the heart of the war has a surreal film noir sentiment to it. The abstract play of light and dark is as effective and powerful as the subject itself."

Act 7

Antony Meets his Cleopatra

Grim-visaged war hath smooth'd his wrinkled front;
And now, instead of mounting barded steeds
To fright the souls of fearful adversaries,
He capers nimbly in a lady's chamber.

(*Shak. Richard III*)

In the spring of 1942 the Army's Intelligence Corps, an arm of MI5, Britain's legendary anti-spy agency, was seeking operatives in Egypt to root out Italian and German agents in the Middle East. Thanks to code-breakers and informants the Nazi espionage machine in Britain had been largely infiltrated and eliminated. On the other hand, Egypt remained a hotbed of foreign spies and subversives, and counterespionage agents were desperately needed to find and arrest them.

The training section of the Intelligence Corps, along with the camouflage unit of Jasper Maskelyne's Magic Gang, were two secret British units concealed within an expansive South African base at Helwan Camp, south of Cairo. Antony successfully passed the Intelligence Corps' training course at the base, learning a range of skills necessary to unearth spies and foreign agents. However, his excellent communication skills made him a natural teacher and, instead of being assigned to the field, he was promoted to corporal and appointed as an instructor at the unit.

There was no entertainment at the camp, other than the bar, so he and many of his colleagues would take a train to Cairo one night a week, assuming they were granted a pass, to enjoy the delights of a city relatively unscathed by the war. Each soldier was permitted just one pass a week, but Antony was a counterespionage instructor; he knew how to slip past the guards and would come and go at will.

One weekend, having sneaked out without a pass on Saturday, he ran into trouble on the Sunday morning when he learned, too late, that there was a compulsory church parade at 8am. It was already 7:45am and he had just fifteen minutes to parade in full kit to be inspected by a senior South African officer. He had no time to press his uniform, bull his boots or clean his rifle – he just scrambled into his crumpled clothes and lined up with the British contingent.

Antony stood in line in the blazing sun for half an hour waiting for the inspecting officer, knowing that he was about to disgrace his regiment and that he risked being severely reprimanded. The heat was rising and Antony's pulse was racing as the parade was called to attention and the inspection began. A single stray hair or a fleck of dandruff on a collar could get a man a severe dressing down or loss of privileges, and Antony watched in trepidation as the officer moved slowly along the line toward him, meticulously inspecting each man as he approached. What would be his punishment? But then…a brainwave. With only seconds to go before his undoing Antony dropped his rifle and crashed face forward onto the sand in a dead faint. "Get that man off the parade ground", yelled the sergeant major, and Antony spent the next half hour in the first-aid hut making a slow and convincing recovery.

Church parades were an annoyance to Antony, as they were to most soldiers, especially as he had no religious beliefs. However, he had discovered that it wasn't wise to reveal such heretical thoughts while belonging to a military steeped in Christian morals and traditions. One soldier who had declared himself an atheist to avoid church parades was made to scrub toilets all day every Sunday, while another had converted from Christianity to Islam and had been forced to kneel on a prayer mat in the scorching sun five times every day.

Antony was frustrated by the situation until his New Zealander friend, Erik, suggested a solution …

Helwan, Egypt
April 1942

Dear Friend

Guess what? I've changed religion.

I was so fed up with wasting every Sunday morning in church when I could have been rehearsing that I put in an application to be a Deist. My adjutant didn't have a clue what a Deist was, so I put him straight and told him that Deists were against all organized religion but still believed in God. Therefore, although I couldn't go to church, I would have to be given every Sunday off to worship by myself. That stumped him.

"*Cudgel thy brains no more about it, for your dull ass will not mend his pace with beating;*" I said, quoting the Clown from Hamlet, but he didn't know what I meant and forwarded my application to the chaplain-general in Cairo. He'd never heard of Deism either so he probably asked God for advice. Anyway, the pair of them were to-ing and fro-ing for weeks before the chaplain-general eventually said that all I really needed was some counseling. What he meant was that I should be dragged, kicking and screaming, back into his fold. My adjutant knew I wouldn't give in easily so he called me into his office, stood me at ease, and said, "Now listen, Holland – Man to man. If I promise not to put you on church parades or fatigues for the rest of your tour, will you give up this Deist crap?" "Yes, Sir!" I said, and I was out of there in a flash.

Antony

The lack of entertainment for the service personnel in Helwan was an irritant to Antony and he decided to fill the void with drama. He had a potential audience of several thousand South Africans, in addition to men from the intelligence and camouflage units, and an all new pool of eager amateur actors – all he needed was a stage. With a bit of sleuthing, he found a vacant hut and got permission to convert it to a theatre. Some Italian prisoners-of-war with carpentry skills were enlisted to help and, in a matter of weeks, the hut was enlarged into a hundred-seat theatre, complete with a stage and dressing room.

It should come as no surprise that Antony's first production was Emlyn Williams' *Night Must Fall* starring none other than Antony Holland in the lead role of Danny. Antony's commanding officer, Major Ormsby, played a small part as the Lord Chief Justice and, as there were no females in the Intelligence Corps, all the actresses came from the South Africans' Sergeants' mess. Sergeant Alice (Kitty) Kitson played the part of the maid. She was apparently besotted by Antony and was constantly nagging her best friend, Gusta Harmon, to see the show and meet him.

"All I heard was, 'Antony this'… 'Antony that'… 'Antony', 'Antony', 'Antony'," claims Gusta, who was eventually so tired of hearing about his virtues that she attended the final night's performance and the subsequent cast party.

Gusta was a sergeant in the South African Women's Auxiliary Army Services and had been with the first group of South African women to serve in Egypt during the war. She was initially in Cairo but didn't like her job and bemoaned the fact to General Adler, an American with the U.S. observer mission, and he offered her a post in his office. She worked for the general for two years, and, due to a bureaucratic anomaly, received a full salary from both the Americans and the South Africans. She then volunteered for a position in Khartoum, Sudan, but developed appendicitis and was shipped back to Egypt to recuperate and ended up in Helwan Camp, compiling statistics on the dead, wounded and missing.

Following the final performance of *Night Must Fall* in the Helwan camp theatre in August 1943, Antony was doing Noel Coward impressions in his dressing gown at the cast party when he grabbed Gusta and started dancing with her. It was a dance that was to last nearly forty years, but it was never destined to be a trouble free waltz in the park.

Sgt. Harmon was very popular among the many male officers at

Helwan, and had such a busy social calendar that she had to include breakfast dates in order to schedule all of her would-be suitors. To complicate matters further for Antony, Gusta was actually engaged to be married to a South African soldier, (although he was on the front lines), and she was also dating Antony's boss – Major Ormsby.

So, why would a popular pin-up girl with a drawer full of proposals accede to Antony's advances? There is no doubt that the twenty three year old intelligence instructor and actor was suave, erudite and charismatic, but he certainly wasn't the lone possessor of those attributes on a large military base. All the same, the single-minded doggedness which had been with him since childhood, and had helped him overcome barriers in his quest for success on the stage, encouraged Antony to pursue Gusta with relentless determination.

Nevertheless, Antony's infatuation with Gusta was, at first, a minor distraction from his theatrical ambitions and he quickly launched into another play by Emlyn Williams, *The Case of the Frightened Lady*, based on a popular crime novel by Edgar Wallace. It too starred Antony Holland in the lead role and was well received, although it lacked the humorous nuggets that had made *Night Must Fall* so popular.

Now Antony felt that his cast and audience were ready for the big step – Shakespeare – and he decided to produce an edited version of *The Merchant of Venice*, keeping all Shylock's scenes intact for himself – naturally!

The amateur actors grasped the nettle and rehearsals went well. A professional make-up artist, who was a member of Maskelyne's camouflage unit, meticulously created Shylock's beard using real hair, while costumes were being made by 'seamstresses' from the South African detachment. Much to the resentment of some of the seamstresses and cast, Antony enlisted Gusta to help with the wardrobe so that he could spend more time with her. As his costume developed, so did their romance. They began using the dressing room at the theatre as a bedroom after rehearsals, and by the time his cloak was finished, and the curtain was about to rise, Antony had finally become a real man.

Just before the show opened a cast member offered to get some flyers widely distributed and, when a plane slowly circled overhead and dropped thousands of leaflets, the camp's Egyptian labourers, who couldn't read English, thought it was the end of the war – it wasn't, but the show was a sell-out and Antony was flying high. He was in love...

Helwan
Egypt
October 1943

Dear Friend

    I am frustrated by a she-devil who taunts me day and night by her beauty and works a thousand ways to rebuff my proposals. "Marry me", I have asked, *ad infinitum,* and she has repeatedly said, "No".

    "Her passions are made of nothing but the finest part of pure love:" as Shakespeare wrote in Antony & Cleopatra. But what would Shakespeare have done if Anne Hathaway had treated his heart with the same disdain that Gusta treats mine? That got me thinking of how alike I am to Shakespeare – not just in my acting and directing skills – but in my personal affairs. When Shakespeare and Anne married she was his senior in years and was socially and financially much more secure, just as Gusta is to me.

    I may be young, penniless, have no qualifications and few prospects, and we certainly couldn't afford a house and servants like she had in South Africa, but in some respects I'm just like Shakespeare – I have big dreams. But Gusta couldn't see the merit of my argument, though I don't know why.

    Romeo was right when he said:

> *"Love is a smoke raised with the fume of sighs;*
> *Being purged, a fire sparkling in lovers' eyes;*
> *Being vex'd a sea nourish'd with lovers' tears:*
> *What is it else? a madness most discreet,*
> *A choking gall and a preserving sweet."*

    My love for Gusta is vex'd and my tears nourish the Nile, but I won't give up. I have searched out fifty of the best love poems ever and I shall read them to her until she agrees to marry me.

Antony

Gusta had turned down very many offers of marriage and she was, in any case, engaged, though neither she nor her South African fiancé seemed in a hurry to tie the knot. Antony, on the other hand, had missed so many opportunities that he seemed desperate. It may have been Antony's protracted poetry readings that led Gusta to agree to marry him, although it is somewhat more likely that she eventually said "Yes" in order to shut him up, with no real intent of keeping her word.

However, as Gusta soon discovered, it is unwise to trifle with the emotions of a desperate man. Within days Antony had placed announcements of their engagement in major newspapers, arranged for the banns to be read, and sent her off to Cairo to buy a diamond engagement ring for herself – he, as usual, having little money.

Now, with Gusta in his pocket, Antony turned back to Shakespeare and was invited to stage his adaptation of *The Merchant of Venice* at a venue called 'Music-for-All' in Cairo. Once again, the performance was very well received and it attracted the attention of an American soldier, Richard Livingstone Coe, who, in civilian life, was drama critic for the Washington Post, but was now writing for Stars and Stripes, the American military newspaper. Coe gave the *Merchant* a glowing review, and even defended the production from a disgruntled audience member who had written to the editor complaining of the cuts that Antony had made.

Coe would later present Antony and Gusta with a wedding gift: a copy of The Oxford Book of Light Verse, in which he wrote:

For Gusta and "Dan"

What do you give a military couple
Taking their vows matrimonial.
Do you give them a drum, a sword or a fife?
Mr. Post. What is the correct ceremonial?

You can't give a house, a vase or a dish
Or the Encyclopedia Britannica.
You must be content with something well meant.
What to do? What to do? Gosh, Oh! Sal Hepatica.

Antony kept this book for nearly seventy years without realizing that Coe had made a joke. The gift he spoke of giving them, Sal Hepatica, was a popular American laxative in the 1940s.

Richard Livingstone Coe returned to America after the war to work for the Washington Post and became one of the Country's leading non-New York theatre critics. He was a knowledgeable advocate of good theatre whose views were regularly solicited by Broadway producers until his death in 1995.

Act 8

Of Triumph ... and Disaster

O, that this too too solid flesh would melt
Thaw and resolve itself into a dew!
Or that the Everlasting had not fix'd
His canon 'gainst self-slaughter! O God! God!
How weary, stale, flat and unprofitable,
Seem to me all the uses of this world!

(Shak. Hamlet)

Antony Holland may have been an excellent actor but, according to Corporal Okely, his business manager in Egypt, he was a lousy soldier who had little respect for the petty strictures of army regulations. So Antony wasn't pleased when he had to ask his commanding officer for permission to marry Gusta Harmon, especially as Major Ormsby had previously dated her. Nevertheless, permission was granted and, as Gusta wanted a church wedding, the ceremony was held in a Baptist church in Cairo in mid November 1943.

Irwin Shaw was the best man at the wedding. He was an American playwright and screenwriter who later wrote many bestselling novels including *The Young Lions* which was eventually made into a Marlon Brando movie. Antony had worked on scenes from Irwin Shaw's antiwar play *Bury the Dead* at Labour Stage before the war and the two had become acquainted in Cairo.

Gusta paid for the wedding, although Antony had scraped enough money together to buy her a gold wedding band, and they set off on their honeymoon to a hotel that had been reserved for them by Shaw.

Hotels in Cairo during the allied campaign were subject to the same discriminatory traditions as the various military messes, this meant that the best hotels were strictly reserved for senior officers and were out of bounds to other ranks. Shaw, being American, was bemused by this archaic rule of the British class system and booked the newlyweds into one of the most luxurious lodges available …

Giza, Egypt.
November 1943

Dear Mum

Married at last! You would have been proud of me in my corporal's uniform. (Actually my own uniform was a bit scruffy so I borrowed one from a friend – a big friend – actually a <u>very</u> big friend. So when you see the photos don't worry – I haven't shrunk).

Gusta thought I looked funny in my baggy outfit, but she married me anyway. She is wonderful.

"I'll say she looks as clear as morning roses newly wash'd with dew:" You will love her. I am so happy.

"O joyful day! I would not take a knighthood for my fortune."

We honeymooned at The Mena House Hotel in Giza and could see the Pyramids from our window. The hotel is very posh and originally was the royal lodge of Khedive Ismail, the man who built The Royal Opera House in Cairo. Even the Prince of Wales stayed here a few years ago.

The funny thing was that after our first night we were asked to stay in our room. We thought it was because we're not commissioned officers and they didn't want riff-raff in the dining room or bar. But the room service was wonderful so we didn't mind. Then on Saturday, when we were leaving, we discovered that the whole place was deserted, we were the only guests and the hotel was completely surrounded by barbed wire fencing, gun emplacements, tanks and armed guards.

I am not allowed to tell you what was happening – but you'll probably read about it in the newspapers.

Antony

The reason for the sizeable military presence at the hotel was later explained when it was announced that Roosevelt, Churchill and Chiang Kai-shek had met in Cairo to discuss the ongoing war. Unbeknownst to Antony and Gusta, their hotel was one of the establishments involved but, as the meeting was not starting until the following Monday, the authorities decided not to disturb the honeymooners while the rest of the building was evacuated and secured.

With the three day honeymoon over the newlyweds returned to Helwan camp to resume normal duties, but within a few weeks their lives turned upside down – Gusta was pregnant. Children had been a contentious issue during the Hollands' whirlwind courtship, with Gusta making it clear that she desperately wanted to have a child. She had in fact terminated her engagement to her previous fiancé because of his refusal to consider children until war's end. But Antony didn't want children either; prophesying that his prospective acting career would not be conducive to rearing a young family – a prophesy that would eventually bear bitter fruit. But he had been determined to marry his Cleopatra whatever the consequences.

The first and, for Antony, most distressing consequence of Gusta's pregnancy was that as soon as her commanding officer learned of the situation she was ordered back to South Africa for formal discharge.

Since Antony's first meeting with Gusta he had been on an emotional rollercoaster as he fought to win her affections, but now, just as he thought he'd hit the lover's jackpot, he suddenly found himself plummeting downhill out of control. With no way of knowing how long the war would last, or whether he would survive it, Antony became maudlin at the thought that he might never again see his wife, and might never hold their child. A severe depression set in, leaving him weeping for hours on end, and he lost all interest in his theatre and his work…

Cairo
April 1943

My dearest wife ... (although I know that I shall never send this letter for fear of worrying you).

Why can Shakespeare put into words emotions that I can only feel?

When Domitius Enobarbus says, *"O sovereign mistress of true melancholy, The poisonous damp of night desponge upon me, That life, a very rebel to my will, May hang no longer on me:"* he is speaking of me. He knows my very soul.

You are gone – *my serpent of the Nile*. When will I see you again?

"Hast thou no care of me? shall I abide
In this dull world, which in thy absence is
No better than a sty?"

I cannot stay here without you and I've asked for a transfer. I see your shadows everywhere. My heart and my theatre lie empty. I have no wish to act, to eat or even to live. As for the black nights that I lay awake without you, as Kent says in Lear, *"Things that love night Love not such nights as these:"*

My heart is with you in South Africa, but this damnable uniform keeps me here. Oh misery! What am I to do?

Your loving husband
Antony

As Antony's depression continued, and deepened, his application for a transfer was eventually granted and he was posted to the Field Security Headquarters in Cairo and given a routine office job.

Although the North African campaign ended in May of 1943, with the Germans' surrender after the battle of El Alamein, the breaking of the Nazi's Enigma codes at Bletchley Park in England uncovered serious security leaks in Cairo. Enemy agents remained active throughout the Middle East and all security units were on high alert to find them. But Antony found it hard to concentrate on his work and was prone to bouts of uncontrollable crying.

Airmail letters arrived regularly from Gusta, and then weeks went by with no word at all. He had no means of telephoning her in South Africa and became evermore distressed and anxious. One morning he didn't return to his office after breakfast, but simply kept walking until he reached the City of the Dead – an enormous cemetery between Cairo and Maadi. This burial ground is laid out as a small city, complete with roads, houses and mosques, where the souls of the dead are believed to exist much as they did in life, and Antony, both emotionally and physically drained, fell into a state of torpor and remained there for several days until he was found by the military police and hospitalized with extreme dehydration.

A batch of letters from Gusta perked him up somewhat and he resumed work although, uncharacteristically, he had no enthusiasm whatsoever to return to the stage. However, that would change when he reconnected with Hassan Fathy, an Egyptian architect whom he had got to know in Maadi.

Hassan and his wife Aziza had lived in a villa on the banks of the Nile when Antony was stationed at the nearby camp, and Antony would spend afternoons at their house enjoying classical music. Now, separated from his wife and living in Cairo, Hassan was writing a play and was hopeful that Antony would produce it for him. Unfortunately for the Egyptian, their first meeting was unproductive as Antony broke down uncontrollably while describing his anguish over Gusta's absence. This emotional display proved a great release for Antony and the following week he, together with Edward Stanley, a British sergeant with a theatre company in Cairo, had dinner with Hassan to discuss the play.

Both Antony and Edward Stanley fell asleep while Hassan read them his play and it never made it to the stage, but the Egyptian's true path lay in building design and he was destined to become a world renowned award-winning architect. However, the relationship with Edward Stanley proved very rewarding for Antony, both at that time and after the war in England. Stanley was a self-taught actor/director who had started a theatre company in Cairo and he asked Antony to direct some plays at 'Music for All' and Cairo University. This invite proved to be the impetus that Antony needed to lift his depression and restore his mental health.

Things picked up further for Antony when ENSA*, a civilian

* ENSA The Entertainments National Service Association.

entertainment company, arrived from England to entertain the troops and needed a leading actor for a two week run of a play called *Black Limelight* at the Ritz Theatre in Cairo. Antony had second billing to Hazel Hughes, an actress who would later make her name in British T.V., and in movies alongside stars like Norman Wisdom, Sophia Loren and David Niven.

However, Antony's reinvigoration was temporary and his spirits sank again when his son, Nelson, was born on August 18, 1944. He had sent a gift – a pillowcase self-embroidered with an African theme – but he felt totally disconnected from the event. It would be eighteen months before he would meet his son, and it's possible that this enforced estrangement may have had lifelong consequences for the father/son relationship.

Antony's emotional rollercoaster got back onto an upswing when he won a transfer to the army's own entertainment unit in Cairo under Captain Torin Thatcher, a former Shakespearean actor at the Old Vic in London, and Antony began directing and starring in repertory at 'Music for All'.

By May of 1945 the war in Europe was over and troops were slowly returning home, but the entertainment unit in Cairo was busier than ever; attempting to amuse the restless troops as they awaited repatriation. It would be some time before Antony could get back to England and he wanted his wife and son there to meet him. The army, however, had different ideas and, despite the fact that they had reunited other military families, initially refused to pay their travel costs. Captain Thatcher went to bat for the young couple and in due course Gusta and their son arrived in England and stayed with Antony's parents ... though not for long.

Meanwhile, Antony was on the first leg of his northward journey home, and he staged plays in Alexandria at a rehab centre for South African soldiers before putting on weekly shows for British soldiers waiting for ships to take them to France. Antony's turn came finally and, after being marooned in Marseille for several weeks while trying to get a train to Paris and the Channel ports, he found himself headed through the lush fields of Provence and he broke down in tears. For the first time in nearly five years he was surrounded by a green and pleasant land that reminded him so much of his youth and all that he had left behind in his native England.

A poignant reminder of home.

Photo – Chandler of Exeter

Antony's mother, Beatrice, sent this picture to him for his twenty second birthday. Dated March 28th 1942.
On the back she wrote, "If ever lost please return to 47, Bampton Street, Tiverton, Devon, England.

Act 9

Peace in Our Time

O, wither'd is the garland of the war,
The soldier's pole is fall'n; young boys and girls
Are level now with men; the odds is gone,
And there is nothing left remarkable
Beneath the visiting moon.

                              (Shak. Antony and Cleopatra)

By the end of 1945 the Second World War was finally over. More than sixty million people had been killed and hundreds of millions mentally and physically disabled, but, despite two close calls in the Blitz of London at the start of the war, Signalman Antony Holland had successfully acted his way through the entire imbroglio without a scratch and without firing a shot in anger. Any mental distress he may have suffered was due to his separation from his wife and newborn son, but as Christmas approached that year he was finally on his way home to reunite with Gusta and to meet eighteen month old Nelson for the first time.

After reporting to his regiment's base camp and arranging for a transfer to the military entertainment's unit known as 'Stars in Battledress' in London, Antony made his way to his hometown in Devon. But Gusta and Nelson were no longer residing with his parents. Gusta had not seen eye to eye with her mother-in-law, Beatrice, and was alarmed by the fact that Antony's father appeared to be physically abusing his wife, so she had taken a secretarial job to pay for independent accommodation soon after arriving in England.

The reunification was not a terrific success. A rushed romance in the heat of the Egyptian desert followed by a hasty marriage, an immediate pregnancy and a long separation, was a poor foundation for a stable relationship, and by the time the young couple were reunited the flame of passion had already died. The war was over and the victory bunting was still blowing in the wind but, by the winter of 1945/6, the privations of the immediate postwar period had cast a distinct chill over Britain and the young Holland family. Gusta was accustomed to a luxurious lifestyle in a middle-class South African home untouched by war: the sun shone all day; the larder was always full; and the household chores were undertaken by servants. England, by comparison, was cold and damp. Food, clothing and fuel were rationed, and affordable servants were impossible to come by. The days of young people entering domestic service had largely died with the advent of military conscription and war service, and the postwar period was a time of social leveling where millions of returning servicemen who had risked their lives defending democracy were no longer willing to accept the autocratic rule of the nobility. The aristocratic Sir Winston Churchill, Britain's victorious wartime prime minister, was ousted from power in 1945 and his Conservative government was replaced by the socialist Labour government of Clement Attlee.

Despite the need to rebuild war ravaged Britain there was mass unemployment as the troops returned and armament related industries closed. Antony's military service was coming to an end and, with his family in tow, he set off to London to work in the office of 'Stars in Battledress' in Grosvenor Square while awaiting demobilization. During this time he was offered various parts entertaining troops in the Far East but, after five years in Egypt and two years separation from Gusta, he turned them all down and, like many of his contemporaries, prepared for an uncertain career on the civilian stage.

When Antony left the army he would be issued with a demob suit but, at a time of austerity when actors were expected to provide their own wardrobes, a single pinstripe suit wouldn't get him far on the London stage. He needed ration coupons to buy a dinner jacket, a sports jacket and a dressing gown, and Terry-Thomas (*Thomas Terry Hoar-Stevens*) latterly one of Britain's best known comic actors, who worked out of the same office as Antony, put him in touch with a black-marketeer. Antony could only afford fifty ration coupons and the spiv laughed at him, saying, "Don't bother me, son. I only deal in thousands". Terry-Thomas wasn't getting what he wanted either. His trademark was his ability to parody pompous military officers and his distinctive voice got him a major role in a BBC* radio series. But he had overlooked the fact that he was still in the armed forces and he stomped around Antony's office in a rage when he learned that all he would get was standard army pay while the war department would get a fat cheque from the BBC.

Peter Ustinov was another private in Antony's office and had spent the war making classic propaganda movies like *One of Our Aircraft is Missing*. Being a private he was required to report for pay parades like everyone else and on one occasion he forgot his uniform cap. He couldn't get his pay without it so he borrowed Antony's. It was much too small for Ustinov, but he perched it on his head and everyone laughed as the pay officer gave him quizzical looks.

With the war over most of the men were just filling in time until demob and they ran all kinds of rackets to make money. A fiscal scandal in Antony's office caused the commanding officer to be replaced by a new C.O., an erstwhile accountant who understood the vagaries of finance but, apparently, not that of men. The Canadian Army band was headed home at that time and in a magnanimous gesture was ordered to donate all of their instruments to 'Stars in Battledress'. The new C.O. instructed Antony's sergeant major to take delivery of the valuable gifts on a Saturday morning as he would be off duty himself and, within minutes of three empty Canadian trucks leaving the depot, a fleet of cars took out hundreds of high quality instruments and returned with a scrap heap of battered old brass. The C.O. was none the wiser when he surveyed the equipment on the following Monday and Antony never discovered what happened to the precious instruments but, forty years later, when he recounted this story in Vancouver, an ex-Canadian bandsman acknowledged being one of the musicians who had reluctantly handed over his trumpet.

Family life for Antony and Gusta in London was hard in the immediate postwar years. Accommodation in London was in short supply because of bomb damage and initially they shared an apartment in Hampstead with two other families. Gusta was soon fed up renting grotty rooms so, for just £100 deposit, they bought a thirty five year lease on a bomb-damaged three story house in Frithville Gardens, Shepherd's

* The British Broadcasting Corporation

Bush, and occupied the centre floor with sitting tenants in the flats above and below. The working-class occupants paid relatively little controlled rent and made it clear that they resented their middle-class landlady, but at least the Hollands now had a permanent roof over their heads and even managed to get the insurance company to pay for the bomb damage.

Finding his feet on the civilian stage after so readily finding an audience among his military colleagues, even stardom in Cairo, was a major problem for Antony and, while Gusta worked as a secretary at the Air Ministry to pay the bills, he spent his days sending query letters and 'doing the rounds' in search of parts.

Labour Stage had not re-opened, but Antony had kept in touch with his teacher and mentor, Nelson Illingworth. The Australian's wife was a director of the recording company, Linguaphone, and had recorded Gielgud reading Dostoevsky's *Crime and Punishment*. Illingworth pulled some strings and got Antony an interview with Gielgud in his dressing room between a matinee and an evening performance. Antony tripped and fell on the carpet as he entered. It was an unusual entrance, but Gielgud wasn't impressed and wasn't at all helpful.

At one point Antony scored an interview with Donald Wolfit, an egotistical actor/manager with a reputation for being cheap. He had started his own touring company in 1937 when none of the established Shakespearean companies would back him, and he generally skimped on costumes and sets and only hired very young or very old actors. Actress Hermione Gingold once said of him, "Olivier is a tour-de-force, but Wolfit is forced to tour".

Antony sat as Wolfit, a relatively small man, walked slowly around sizing him up before suggesting that he could only offer the part of a dwarf. Antony was five feet eleven inches and concluded that Wolfit suffered from small man syndrome in addition to an over-inflated ego.

Illingworth tried again, this time with the producer of a repertory company in Hayes, Middlesex, which attracted agents looking for talent to become stars in London's West End. Antony's query letter to the female producer had been ignored, but as she had been a student of Illingworth he called her and insisted that she should give Antony an audition. She agreed, and Antony spent a solid week learning different parts. He walked in, gave his name and without looking up she said, "Are you free next week?" No audition or questions, and he was given a tiny part in a one week run of Harold Brighouse's *Hobson's Choice*. That was it – she had paid her debt to Illingworth and Antony had got nowhere near the West End.

Illingworth also tried to cure Antony's youngest brother, Kaye, of a persistent stammer – that hadn't worked either.

Finally, in 1946, Antony landed a job with the West of England Theatre Company based in Exmouth, in his home county of Devon, performing three-weekly repertories.

Repertory theatre was demanding, grueling and unrewarding, with actors simultaneously performing one play while rehearsing for the next. The actors were generally ambitious youngsters hoping to make their way up the ladder to London's West End or faded stars on their way back down. Repertory troupes were small, just seven or eight actors which included a leading man and leading lady, juvenile male and female (the ingénue), and male and female character actors who played older roles. Actors often played several parts in different acts of the same play while the smallest roles would frequently be taken by stage crew or by local amateurs. The dreadful hours, conditions and pay of repertory companies are still infamous today and only the most passionate or desperate actors would survive for long.

The West of England Theatre was particularly demanding because the company would perform throughout the entire south west of the country. Each morning the cast would rehearse in Exmouth for the upcoming play then drive up to two hours to the venue for that day's presentation. And, late at night, following the performance, they would drive back to Exmouth for a few hours sleep before the next morning's rehearsal. Sundays would be spent learning lines.

For publicity purposes, repertory companies often employed actors based on their 'name' and not necessarily their abilities. Godfrey Bond was the West of England's leading man and his main claim to fame was that he had appeared with John Gielgud as Capulet's cousin in Shakespeare's *Romeo and Juliet* at The Manchester Opera House in 1935. However, Bond had acted little during the intervening war years. He was rusty; he couldn't remember his lines and he was often late for his entrances. For instance, during the West of England's 1946 production of *Macbeth*, featuring Alex Dunn as Macbeth, Godfrey Bond as Banquo, and Antony Holland in the dual roles of Lennox and Ross, each time that Macbeth went onstage supposedly in conversation with Banquo, Alex

Dunn would be talking to himself until someone gave Bond a hefty shove from the wings.

During one of Bond's belated entrances a woman in the gods stood up and screamed "There's Jesus Christ" just as he came onstage. Bond completely froze and couldn't recover. He went offstage cursing and swearing, although he returned after a costume change. But the woman wasn't fooled and yelled "There's Jesus again". Bond froze for the second time and the heckler was ejected, but he was terrified of going on for the rest of the show.

Another problem for the company was that the actor playing Duncan and MacDuff was almost totally blind. He was an old friend of the manager and needed work, but he would stumble about the stage, bashing into props, scenery and other actors. The show got very bad reviews, although one critic cheered Antony by saying, "The young man playing Lennox and Ross was the only one who was any good".

Lady Macbeth was played by the manager's wife, Canadian actress Joyce Worsley, who much later had small parts in films like *Tootsie* and *Grace Quigley* as well as the popular American TV cop series, *Cagney and Lacy*.

Godfrey Bond's wife, Mavis Edwards, was also an actress with the West of England Company and, despite the obvious age disparity, Antony often played a father to her character. However, Mavis had a Machiavellian streak when it came to stealing the limelight ....

Exmouth
August 1946

Dear Friend

Women! Women! Women!

I ask you... what did the Clown say to Cleopatra about women?

"*I know that a woman is a dish for the gods, if the devil dress her not. But, truly, these same whoreson devils do the gods great harm in their women; for in every ten that they make, the devils mar five.*"

Precisely ... and this week I have been harmed greatly by a devilish whore named Mavis Edwards. Picture me... I am the great statesman Benjamin Disraeli in Housman's 'Victoria Regina'. It's not a big part, although I also play the Archbishop of Canterbury, but at least I have great dialogue. So I milked it. After my stirring patriotic speech as Disraeli I would toast the Queen, smash the glass triumphantly into the fireplace, bow almost to the ground and back out – always to thunderous applause. As York says in Richard II, "*...the eyes of men, after a well-graced actor leaves the stage, are idly bent on him that enters next, thinking his prattle to be tedious:*"

So last night when a director from Bristol Old Vic came to see the show, looking for talent for his new theatre company, like Iago in Othello I said to myself, "*This is the night that either makes me or fordoes me quite.*"

Well, I pulled out all the stops, but so did Mavis. As I readied to bow at the end of Disraeli's speech the scheming bitch deliberately dropped her crown jewels with a clatter onto the stage. I couldn't believe it... as I smashed my glass, bowed deeply and backed gracefully into the wings, there was Queen Victoria scrabbling around on the stage with the Bristol director and two hundred pairs of eyes firmly glued to her bum. No one even noticed my exit!

Mark my words – Working with animals and kids might be tricky, but working with Mavis Edwards can be a whole lot trickier.

Antony

Antony's early successes in the theatre, both as a director and an actor, had largely been self-generated, but, while his strategy of forming amateur companies to provide a vehicle for his talent had certainly served his purpose at the time, it was not a financially sound model. On the other hand, despite the obvious shortcomings, repertory theatre offered a pay cheque and, more importantly for someone as passionate about acting as Antony, the chance of being spotted by an agent for one of the national or provincial theatre companies. The missed opportunity to be chosen for the Bristol Old Vic was therefore quite a blow and compelled Antony to continue in rep.

His next job was in Scotland doing fortnightly rep – a new play to learn every two weeks – with some presentations in Perth, while the others were performed on the stage of the Adam Smith Hall, Kirkcaldy: a town with a linoleum factory that created an all-pervading stink. And the following summer he returned to the West of England Company while Gusta stayed in London to have their second child. At that time she was working as a typist for celebrated Shakespearean critic and academic (George) Wilson Knight. It was said by some that Knight could write ten pages about every line of Shakespeare and, unfortunately, he often did. Canadian actor, producer and critic, James Mavor Moore, was taught by Knight in Toronto in the 1930s and he once said to Antony, "Knight has the ability to turn a tragedy to a comedy and a comedy to a tragedy".

Knight once critiqued Antony's Shylock and complained that he should have carried a cane and that his voice did not have the necessary rise and fall. Despite Knight's notoriety, Antony was not impressed and concluded that the revered critic was a charlatan realising that Knight's judgment was entirely based on a portrait of a cane-wielding Sir Henry Irving and the well-known fact that nineteenth century Shakespearean actors spoke in a sing-song manner.

Rep was hard both on Antony and on his family, and wasn't at all lucrative. He worked excessively long hours and was away from home for long periods and, although Gusta was having a very difficult pregnancy, she had to keep working, typing at home, to support the family. Antony's wages were measly and he had to pay for his board and lodging and travel, but when Gusta complained about her difficulties Antony responded unsympathetically, saying, "You're pregnant, you haven't got a disease".

The Holland's second child, a daughter named Rosheen after Antony's pre-war 'mother' and landlady at Labour Stage, was born on October 12, 1947, but, while her birth may have relieved Gusta of the pain of pregnancy, life in postwar London wasn't about to improve for the struggling actor and his South African wife.

Act 10

Bristol Old Vic

And then the justice,
In fair round belly with good capon lined,
With eyes severe and beard of formal cut,
Full of wise saws and modern instances;

(Shak. As You Like It)

The Theatre Royal Bristol is the oldest working theatre in Great Britain. It has been in more or less continuous use since May 30, 1766, when the distinguished Georgian actor and playwright, David Garrick, opened it with a prologue. It is now a Grade 1 listed building of exceptional historic value and it has been the home of the Bristol Old Vic Theatre Company (BOV) for over half a century.

The BOV was formed in 1945 by a troupe of celebrities seconded from the London Old Vic, and the early players included Dorothy Tutin, John Neville and Peter O'Toole. The BOV produced its first play (Farquhar's *The Beaux' Stratagem*) at the Theatre Royal Bristol on February 19, 1946, and on October 21 that same year Laurence Olivier opened the Bristol Old Vic Theatre School as an adjunct to the company, but, unlike the Theatre Royal itself, the school was impressive in name only and actually occupied a large room above an old fruit and vegetable warehouse belonging to Powell Harvey & Co. in nearby Queen Charlotte Street. Olivier gave the inaugural speech from the stage of the Theatre Royal and never actually visited the school's premises. To have done so might have meant squeezing past sacks of cauliflowers, cabbages and potatoes in order to climb the creaky staircase to the shabby wooden-floored classroom where he could have been bowled over by the stench of rotting onions and mouldy oranges that regularly permeated from the warehouse below.

The Victorian redbrick building, in a cobbled street bustling with vegetable merchants' barrow boys, was totally unsuitable for a theatre school, but vacant property in Bristol was scarce due to severe bomb damage and, in any case, the school was grossly underfunded and couldn't afford better.

The first Principal of the Bristol Old Vic Theatre School (BOVTS) was an ex-soldier named Edward Stanley, whom Antony had known in Egypt, who had been directing and acting in Cairo throughout the war with a group called the New Vic Players. It is not known how Stanley came to be heading up the new school in Bristol as he had no professional theatrical accreditations or qualifications whatsoever; in fact he was a self-confessed amateur who proudly proclaimed that he had never had a day's training in his life. But Stanley was a magnetically charming man with a resonant voice, and he wasn't alone if he had overstated his experience to secure the post. Even Antony Holland could embroider his *curriculum vitae* on occasion, and at least one program featuring Antony implies, falsely, that he studied at the Royal Academy of Dramatic Art in London. Actors, by definition, are people who excel at convincing others that they are someone they are not, and they are generally people who have successfully done so from early childhood. Scratch any actor and you will almost certainly find another actor underneath!

Antony Holland is, and always was, such a dyed in the wool actor, and he would eventually find his way to the Bristol Old Vic Theatre School as Edward Stanley's assistant, but only after several more taxing years in repertory theatre that would have dispirited a less determined man. Today, Antony's daughter, Rosheen, says of her father's unwavering dedication to the stage, "He knew exactly what he wanted to do from the earliest age. He was born to it. I never picked up the slightest vacillation; never the slightest doubt – ever. He never compromised and he stuck to his path whatever. It drove my mother mad."

Antony consistently drove his wife mad by his refusal to get a 'real job' and the situation was not improved by the fact that, while Gusta spent her evenings at home looking after two young children, Antony was often far away apparently enjoying himself in the company of other women. Rosemary Harris was a case in point when Antony was appearing in twice-nightly rep in Bedford. The show was Ian Hay's comedy *The Sport of Kings,* starring Wally Patch (one of Britain's most prolific yet least known movie actors), and there were two performances each evening with just half an hour turnaround in between. The ASM* was Rosemary Harris and Antony was totally enamoured by her. She was not only very beautiful, but she hung on his every word as she gazed adoringly into his eyes during the intermission. Nothing would have come of this apparently mutual adoration had they not met again several years later when working together in Bristol. The pair shared meals together and Antony was so besotted by Rosemary that he, perhaps unwisely, told Gusta about her. However, the potentially marriage-ending situation was quickly resolved when Antony saw that Rosemary looked at the show's technical director with the same rapt expression.

Rosemary Harris has been a movie and Broadway star for more than fifty years and Antony met her again when she was in her early sixties. He says, with a note of resignation, "She seemed to have lost interest in me – she was only interested in herself."

After his experiences of repertory theatre in Exmouth, Perth and Bedford, Antony was tired of being away from his family; tired of the poor pay; and tired of the relentless grind, and vowed that if he had to continue doing it for a living he would give it up. Nevertheless, in 1949, he was back onstage, this time in Cromer, Norfolk, for the summer season of rep at The Town Hall Theatre.

Cromer is one of a number of east coast seaside resorts in England that were made fashionable during the Victorian era. The opening of the railway from London in 1877 brought the masses escaping the capital's polluted streets, if only for a week each summer, and ensured a constant turnover of patrons for the repertory theatre. In the gloomy postwar period holidaymakers wanted light entertainment, so the chosen plays were formulaic; generally three-act comedies with a single set and eight performers, and they changed every Thursday so that visitors arriving each weekend could catch two different shows during their stay. However, one-week rep was particularly demanding as actors would be performing one play while simultaneously rehearsing for the next and even learning the lines for a third ... if the scripts had arrived in time.

*Assistant Stage Manager

Photo – Anon

Antony as 'Bill' in the 1927 play *Trespass* by Emlyn Williams at Cromer Town Hall Theatre, (1951)

Life wasn't easy for Gusta in London while Antony was working in Cromer. "For better for worse, for richer for poorer", she had vowed on her marriage to Antony, and she would stick to that promise, but there is no question that she felt somewhat betrayed and hurt because of what she had given up in South Africa for a difficult life in war weary England. She was taking care of two young children while working to support Antony's poorly paid theatrical career and even had to do the family's laundry in an old washtub – although she finally rebelled and refused to do the laundry until Antony bought her a washing machine. One answer was for Gusta to join her husband on the coast for the summer and Antony borrowed a camper van from his prewar girlfriend, Brenda Pool, enabling his family to stay near him in Cromer.

The plays were a real slog; learning and rehearsing one while performing another and changing every Thursday, and all for £8 a week. However, at the end of the summer season in 1949 things began to look brighter. Because Antony had to stay in Cromer throughout the busiest season even the most basic accommodation, a shabbily furnished room above a greasy-spoon café, had taken the lion's share of his wages, so he had turned down a contract for the following summer. But the theatre's management had other ideas and offered him a pay rise to return as the director. Antony agreed, and then he heard that the Principal of the Bristol Old Vic Theatre School was looking for an assistant ...

Bristol Old Vic Theatre School
27 Queen Charlotte Street
Bristol
December 1949

From the desk of the Assistant Principal, A.E.Holland

Dear Friend

Finally – a regular pay cheque and Gusta is happy.

Edward Stanley is the Principal. I hadn't seen him since Cairo in 1945. The classroom is above a greengrocer's and the students tell me they call it 'The Fruit School.' I thought at first they were referring to the odour that constantly permeates the building, but then I wondered if they meant the teachers. I must admit that the staff are a little odd – enthusiastic amateurs mainly – and they remind me of characters in a Noel Coward comedy. Edward Stanley is the smooth-talking lothario with Brylcreamed hair, usually seen wearing a silk dressing gown while postulating with his cigarette, whose acting process is based entirely on Coward's method – *'Speak clearly, don't bump into the furniture and if you must have motivation think of your pay packet on Friday.'* He even brags about his total lack of training.

Isabel Chisman is the matron – a rather sweet but frighteningly large woman who wears black tights and an awful wig. She teaches mime and terrifies the young men by insisting that they should lift her into the air as she demonstrates technique.

Edith Manvell teaches voice – and she certainly has the tongue for it – while Rudi Shelley is a homosexual Austrian dancer who teaches movement and spends a lot of time focusing on the boys' bottoms while encouraging them to, 'squeeze their lemons'. Whatever that means!

I would mention 'Stanislavski' but fear that no one would have heard of him.

Antony

Despite Edward Stanley's lack of professional training, he was certainly aware of Stanislavski's method.* However, when interviewed about the school's philosophy for 'Theatre World' in 1947 he had given a rambling answer, saying that the school subscribed to no particular dogmatic teaching of convention, movement, acting or thought, and simply aimed to help each student become a 'sensitive instrument sensitized by every means we know of or can develop, balanced and controlled by a live and exploring mind, seeking always true harmony of thought, feeling and technical expression.'**

Antony was the only trained professional at BOVTS at this time and was an advocate of Stanislavski. However, he later became more skeptical of the Russian's dogmatic acting method, especially when he discovered that Stanislavski had eventually moved away from his own teachings.

In addition to assisting Edward Stanley in the day-to-day administration of the school, Antony taught acting, stage fighting, stage management, and fencing. Most lessons were given in the classroom above the fruit and veg merchant's warehouse. It was sparsely equipped with an upright piano, chairs, lockers for the students' books and swords, and a single toilet. Early productions of the school were presented in the classroom, often with most of the audience sitting on the bare wooden floor, while crowd scenes and stage fights were rehearsed in the adjacent yard of a derelict church school which was also the venue for Antony to teach his specialty – fencing.

One of Antony's first students was Norman Rossington, who was to have a glittering career with the Royal Shakespeare Company and the New York Met., and would appear in numerous movies, including many of the *Carry On* series, The Beatles' *A Hard Day's Night*, and *Double Trouble* starring Elvis Presley. Norman Rossington died in 1999, but one of his cohorts and another luminary of the British stage and screen, Phyllida

---

*Constantin Stanislavski's method, (greatly simplified), taught that an actor must deeply analyze his character's motivations and have a perfect understanding of the character's objective in each scene as well as the "super objective" of the entire play. The Stanislavski 'system' demanded a psycho-physical union where the body displays the inner thoughts and expresses the emotions. However, it has severe limitations. For instance, Russian actors would spend three or four years rigorously researching and rehearsing a part in a Chekhov play in order to experience the right emotions.

**From: Bristol Old Vic Theatre School *the first 50 years 1946 – 1996.* by Shirley Brown.

Law, has many memories of Antony and her time at the theatre school in the early fifties.

Originally from Glasgow, Phyllida had been evacuated during the war and ended up in a senior school in Bristol – a potentially unwise move as Bristol ultimately became the fifth most heavily bombed British city. However, being away from home gave her the freedom to go to the theatre, something she was unable to do in Glasgow as her grandmother was convinced that theatre was the work of the devil.

A performance of Shakespeare's *King Lear* at Bristol Old Vic so moved Phyllida that she absentmindedly walked into a lamppost on the way home and from that moment was determined to go onstage – not as an actress, but as a set designer. Her first year of the two year technical course at BOVTS began with acting and basic theatre, together with fencing. "Women don't fence in Shakespeare", she had protested, but as Antony was running the course everybody had to fence, even Gusta. "The Hollands were very keen on fencing," says Phyllida, "They used to fence everywhere – even in the kitchen."

To Phyllida, a petite nineteen year old at that time, Antony was an imposing figure who appeared immensely tall. "He always wore a huge overcoat and loped like a figure stepping out of a Lowry painting," she says, adding with obvious admiration, "He was a silent creature with a strong jaw which gave him an evil grin, and he would sit with his legs crossed and his arms folded in a theatrical pose and just listen. He was a man of few words, especially at mock auditions where he would sit at a table and never raise his eyes. It was very disconcerting, as it was meant to be. He wouldn't look up and wouldn't say anything. It was as if he was challenging you to make him look at you – but he never did."

Antony's disarming auditioning practices became legendary, both at Bristol and much later in Vancouver, but Phyllida Law's most enduring memory of him at BOVTS was his magnetic attraction of women. "He was always surrounded by women – especially much younger women," she says and, after a moment's thought, adds in her distinctly polished British accent that is evocative of her roles in movies such as *Peter's Friends, Emma,* and *Nanny McPhee,* "Antony was an absolute killer for the birds."

Another of Antony's students from his early years at BOVTS was Lisa Sibley (now Lisa Hoghton) who recalls Antony as a disciplinarian who would punish anyone caught chatting during class by challenging them to a five minute sabre fight. Girls didn't usually fight with sabres so it was best not to be caught. However, Lisa enjoyed both epée and foil and, under Antony's tutelage, entered the West of England Fencing Championships. To Antony's amazement she came second. Lisa never needed her fencing skills in the theatre but, before giving up the stage to become an air hostess, she appeared in the 1954 classic comedy *The Belles of St. Trinians.*

Retired actress Gillian Beton recalls Antony as being terribly dramatic at BOVTS, but it was his sensible practical advice that enabled her to survive in the business at a time when thousands of actors were vying for roles. She stayed in theatre and in television for many years, and deputized for Dorothy Tutin in one long-running show. Antony also taught her to fence and she achieved success in the Gloucester Fencing Championships with the foil.

Antony had learned to fence in Cairo during the war in a school run by a very good French swordsman. But Antony's lessons were generally with an Egyptian who didn't speak English and who taught the Italian style of foil. The Egyptian teacher wasn't at all forgiving in their contests, possibly because he recognized the British as an occupying army and was vengeful. But stiff competition leads to fast learning in battle and Antony soon developed the techniques. On the other hand, the language barrier prevented him from learning the theory. However, the French style of fencing, not the Italian, is commonly used in British theatre, so in order to teach at BOVTS Antony had to take lessons just to stay one step ahead of his students.

Antony trained many award winning competitive fencers over the years, including one by the name of Jerome Silberman of Milwaukee, Wisconsin, who would later adopt a stage name and become Gene Wilder.

Silberman arrived from America thinking that he could fence, until Antony took him on, and in a lengthy letter to Antony, dated April 8, 1956, Wilder explains how much Antony's teachings have improved his style. The letter concludes with a personal note of thanks to Antony and Gusta for their kindness and help during his time in Bristol, writing, "The funny thing about most typical Englishmen is that most of them aren't very typical". Thanks to Antony, Jerome Silberman won the All-School's Fencing Championships on his return to America and subsidized his early acting career by teaching fencing.

Despite all his acting and fencing skills, Antony Holland was never destined to become an international star like Gene Wilder, but he did become the Honorary Secretary of the Gloucester Amateur Fencing Union.

Antony finally gave up fencing in his mid eighties. He claims, tongue in cheek, that he read somewhere that fencing caused certain overworked muscles to become particularly enlarged, and so he worried that if he kept up his fencing into his nineties he might end up with an overdeveloped right arm.

Antony's relatively secure position at BOVTS in 1950 enabled the family to let their London flat and move to Bristol where they were able to spend more time together. However, the chasm that had developed twixt father and son in the first eighteen months of Nelson's life seems only to have widened during the years that Antony had spent in rep.

Irene, Antony's youngest brother's wife, knew the family in London soon after the war when she was a dancer at The London Palladium as a member of the glamorous, high-kicking, troupe known as 'The Tiller Girls'. She had met her husband, Kaye Holland (then on leave from the Merchant Navy) while babysitting for Gusta and Antony, and today she says, "I used to tell Antony that he was a lousy father. Nelson was an adorable child but both his parents were self-absorbed. They weren't good parents."

In some ways Antony's daughter, Rosheen, echoes her aunt's critical view, explaining that while her father was there for her and her brother, in many ways he wasn't, saying, "His mind was always on the theatre. He was so busy that I was allowed to be myself. I don't know whether that was good or bad but it permitted me to evolve and grow into my own person."

However, Nelson appears to have reacted differently to this 'hands-off' approach to parenting. He was a sickly child who suffered with asthma and missed a lot of school and, to people beyond his immediate family, he seemed vulnerable. He once asked his Aunt Irene, "Why do adults hate me?"

The rift between Antony and his son has never properly healed, and has sometimes been played out in the public arena. Christopher Gaze, an alumnus of the Bristol Old Vic Theatre School and the Artistic Director and driving force behind Vancouver's wildly successful annual Shakespearean festival 'Bard on the Beach', recalls a moving incident in

2002 when he was playing the 'Fool' in a staged reading of *King Lear* at Christ Church Cathedral, Vancouver, as part of John Juliani's Shakespeare's Project. Antony was playing the leading role of Lear when, at the end of the performance, a man was heard loudly sobbing in the back row. A voice asked, "Are you all right?" and through the sobs the man replied, "That's my father".

Phyllida Law, who got to know the family well in the early fifties, probably sums up the situation best when she says, "Nelson was a very serious young boy with spectacles who was attempting to bring his parents up."

Photo — Anon. Courtesy Bristol Old Vic

Antony as the Wizard in the pantomime, Jack and the Beanstalk, at the Theatre Royal Bristol
(circa 1954)

Act 11

A Bit of a Pantomime

*A*ll *the world's a stage,*
And all the men and women merely players:
They have their exits and their entrances;
And one man in his time plays many parts,
(Shak. As You Like It)

Christmas pantomimes have been a staple of English theatre since the early 1800s. These frolicking shows are most often based on popular fairytales and combine music, song, dance, cross-dressing, slapstick, sexual innuendo, toilet humour and topical comedy into a family entertainment that operates on many levels. Equity, the actors' union, regularly permitted six students from BOVTS (two backstage and four actors) to participate in productions of the Bristol Old Vic in the 1940s and 1950s, and the annual pantomime was a time when everyone wanted to be involved.

Antony's most vivid memory of pantomime at Bristol is of a performance of *Jack and the Beanstalk* when he was nearly killed onstage by a Meccano submarine and a student named David Larder ...

The Bristol Old Vic.
December 1952

Dear Friend

I'm the Evil Wizard in the panto again this year, although it was almost my last year thanks to David Larder.

He was the front end of the panto cow at first – until the girl in the back complained that he kept farting and he was replaced. But the idiot had messed up the control wires for the eyes, ears and mouth, so every time the cow spoke she would blink furiously, and then she'd open her mouth to hear the reply. The audience roared with laughter, but the director was so ticked off that he put Larder in the wings and gave him one simple job – all he had to do was to hook the wire onto my coat for my big scene... a rousing speech downstage, then with a flash-bang my wizard's coat and hat would be yanked into the air by the wire and I would be revealed as a shady Spiv. And then the trapdoor would open under me and I would drop out of sight in a puff of smoke – Poof!

Anyhow, Nelson had a Meccano set for Christmas and I was doing a bit of intricate engineering on a really awesome submarine in my dressing room last night when I missed my two-minute call – it could happen to anyone. I raced to the wings just as my intro music started but in my panic I'd forgotten my Spiv's tie, so Larder whipped off his own tie and put it on me. But the stupid bugger hooked it onto the wire that was going to yank off my Wizard's coat and hat. I couldn't see what he'd done, so I said my piece, stepped onto the trap and waited for the bang and the smoke...

Luckily I felt the noose tightening around my neck and just as the trap opened I flung myself off. Two seconds more and I would have been lynched ... As Hamlet says, *"tis the sport to have the engineer hoist with his own petard:"*

Yep ... I'm still working with damned amateurs.

Antony

Rosheen, Antony's daughter, once saw her father in the role of the wizard in the Christmas panto at The Theatre Royal and was taken to visit him in his dressing room after the show. It should have been a happy moment, but the young girl couldn't understand why he had apparently lost his magical powers. She wanted to see him replicate the tricks he had done onstage with the help of special effects – she wanted to see him disappear in a puff of smoke – and when he couldn't she became absolutely inconsolable.

David Larder didn't last long at BOVTS after his near-fatal mistake, but he wasn't alone in being shown the door. The school offered places to twenty four new students each year, but only the best twelve were allowed to continue into the second year. This somewhat stringent policy was essential to fulfill the school's mandate of providing a practical education that would prepare students for a demanding vocation in the theatre – something that it succeeded in doing very well.

Christopher Gaze, who studied at BOVTS from 1970 to 1973, is just one of the thousands of graduates who attributes his highly successful theatrical career to his time at the school. As he says, "Bristol was well respected as a school of classical theatre, while many others at the time were avant-garde."

Antony knew from personal experience that graduates would be entering the most challenging of professions: the job opportunities were limited and fiercely contested; the working hours and conditions were Dickensian; and the financial rewards were often pitiful. Only the most passionate, talented and dedicated would survive in the real world. So the fierce competition to remain in the course after the first year was a good way to weed out incompetent or less committed students.

Some of Antony's best students also had an opportunity to gain practical experience by working for him in one-week summer rep. Phyllida Law, Norman Rossington and Kenneth Cope (all ultimately to become household names in the world of British television and film) began their working careers under Antony at Cromer, and learnt the hard way about the unmerciful life on the stage.

In addition to directing at Cromer, Antony was also the stage manager, the administrator and the lighting technician. With a new play every week, the schedule for the whole crew was grueling. Scripts would arrive for the following show a few days early and Antony had to read them, cast them, and decide on scenery and props. Rehearsals would begin each Thursday morning with a read through and blocking, followed by a few hours for the actors to learn lines before going onstage with the current production. Rehearsals for each of the three acts of the upcoming play were held on Saturday, Monday and Tuesday, while Sunday was dedicated to learning the new lines. But every evening, bar Sunday, the cast would be back onstage performing the present play.

The scripts came from London – sometimes late – and one set arrived so late that Antony had to cast the play, block it and do the first rehearsal before he'd even read it. But Antony was tough on the actors and wouldn't normally start directing until people knew their lines. The odd television actor got fired because they weren't used to learning lengthy pieces, but most of the actors were familiar with rep and had no trouble.

After the curtain came down every Wednesday night, the set from the previous show was struck and the new one built, and then Antony would position the lights for the next play. The stage had to be ready, and the lighting cues scripted for the ASM, so that the actors could begin the dress rehearsal on Thursday morning and be ready to open the show that same evening.

The theatre at Cromer had two and half sets of flats* and every play had to have a different scene because some patrons would see two shows in one week. The set designer and decorator was a minor member of the aristocracy, Sir Anthony Denny, who worked in a cramped space under the stage – painting the scenery sideways because there wasn't room to stand the flats upright.

Phyllida Law was an ASM at Cromer under Antony's direction and operating the lights during the performance was only one of her many jobs. First she had to beg and borrow props and furniture from local businesses to set the stage – sometimes an awkward task because not everything had been returned in previous years – and then she was responsible for making sure that the actors were properly dressed and had the right props, and that everything, and everyone, got on and off stage at the right time. She also had to operate any special effects. For instance, in Mary Chase's play, *Harvey*, Phyllida had to lie on the floor and work the light switches with her feet while opening and closing a trap door and pushing a stuffed rabbit on and off stage.

---

*Large plywood boards that form the back and sides of the set onstage.

Photo — Anon

Antony as 'Elwood Dowd' in *Harvey*, with shadow of stuffed rabbit operated by Phyllida Law. (1950)

Phyllida was good at finding props, and creating scenes, and on completing her course at the school she spent two years as a scene painter at Bristol's Theatre Royal with the BOV Company. She then designed costumes for a ballet company for awhile before finally getting into acting, she says, "By mistake." However, it was a 'mistake' that would eventually delight millions of television viewers and moviegoers.

The main competition for the theatre in Cromer was the music hall concert parties and *Summer Seaside Specials* in the Pavilion at the end of the pier. But the pier had another attraction for Antony – a lifeboat station with a long steep ramp down to the sea. The lifeboat launch was a

97

spectacular affair, with the boat, its crew on deck in oilskins, rushing headlong down the ramp and diving headfirst into the sea …

Cromer
August 1952

Dear Friend

Sir Tony and I were putting up the new set at about 3am this morning when we heard some huge explosions. "I hope that's not the blasted Jerries again," I joked, but it wasn't. It was maroons summoning the lifeboat crew. We dropped everything and ran to wake up Norman and Kenneth so they could come and watch.

"Once more unto the breach, dear friends, once more." I yelled as I hammered on their door, "The lifeboat's going out...The lifeboat's going out." There was a moment's silence, and I was just about to bang again when one of them threw a shoe at me and shouted, "Fuck off."

"Your loss," I said and raced with Tony to the end of the pier.

What a sight! The station doors were wide open and the lifeboat, with its giant engines throbbing, stood at the top of a giant ski ramp waiting to plunge into the ocean's boiling fury far below. A dozen men in oilskins and sou'westers were clambering aboard while a shoreman readied to let slip the chains. As he made his move I jumped onto an old fish box and in the immortal words of Shakespeare's Henry V, I exhorted them to great acts of heroism.

I raised my right arm in salute and I cried: *"I see you stand like greyhounds in the slips, Straining upon the start. The game's afoot: Follow your spirit, and upon this charge, Cry "God for Harry, England, and St. George!"*

With these words, the lifeboat began its descent and the coxswain grabbed the wheel and raised his voice above the howling wind to tell me to 'fuck off' as well. Some people can be so ungrateful.

Antony

98

A few weeks after the lifeboat's launch, following the season's final night party, Norman Rossington and Kenneth Cope got revenge on Antony for disturbing their sleep. Antony was completely exhausted after three solid months of work and had gone to bed as soon as the last performance was over. At 3am the following morning Norman and Kenneth began hammering on his door, shouting, "Antony...Antony. Wake Up". Antony woke with a start, terrified that some disaster had occurred. "What is it – a fire?" he demanded. "No", they said, "It's the lifeboat – It's coming back".

Photo - Anon

Antony as 'Crocker Harris'. with Michael Reddington, in Terrence Rattigan's *The Browning Version* Cromer Town Hall Theatre, (1952).

With another season of rep over, Antony returned to Bristol to greet the eager freshmen arriving to audition for the new term. The competition was fierce; many came but few were chosen. However some foreign students, especially Canadians and Americans, were accepted solely on recommendation from their universities.

One couple from wealthy Californian homes was so shocked at the living conditions in Bristol that they didn't stay long. But another American, Gene Wilder, would become a world famous stage and movie star. While Wilder is universally known for his Oscar nominated role in *The Producers* and his Golden Globe nominated role as Willy Wonka, in the film adaptation of Roald Dahl's *Charlie and the Chocolate Factory*, few people realize that he started his career as a Shakespearean actor, studying first at the University of Iowa and then in 1955 at the BOVTS under Antony Holland.

Roger Gage was another of Antony's students who went on to have an illustrious career as an actor and television director. However, Gage is best known as the first husband of multi-award-winning actress Joan Plowright. Antony trained Gage in competitive fencing in Bristol and worked with him on the choreography of a major scene for the BOV Company's *Macbeth*. The young actress, Joan Plowright, had studied at the Old Vic School in London and had joined the Bristol company where she would watch Antony and Gage practicing their fencings. One day in 1953 Joan invited Antony and Roger Gage to see Laurence Olivier in the movie of *The Beggar's Opera*. They went together, but Antony ended up playing gooseberry as Plowright was clearly much more interested in Roger Gage than she was in Olivier. The couple married in September 1953, but by 1961 they were divorced and Joan Plowright finally got the man in the movie: Sir Laurence Olivier.

Postscript: In 2000 an English theatre company was appearing in Nanaimo, British Columbia, and Antony was asked to show them around Gabriola Island. Joan Plowright's daughter, Julie Kate Olivier, was one of the visitors, and Antony delighted in telling her of his association with her mother.

A turning point came for BOVTS in May of 1954 when Edward Stanley left under something of a cloud. Charles Landstone writes in his book, *The Bristol Old Vic, the first ten years,* that, "Edward Stanley kept the school going in 'a wonderful happy muddle' for eight years despite great difficulties: the premises and facilities were inadequate; the staff were underpaid and, in some cases, inexperienced or inefficient; and Denis Carey, who took over from Hugh Hunt as Principal of the BOV Company in 1950, had 'frankly never taken a very great interest in it'".

Shirley Brown, author of, *Bristol Old Vic Theatre School, the first fifty years,* comments on Stanley's resignation, quoting Landstone, and referring to a damaging rift between the Principal and Antony, his assistant, as an aggravating concern.

The degree to which Stanley kept the school going is a matter of some conjecture. He was the Principal, but he spent much of his time directing local amateur groups, invigilating amateur competitions and giving lectures off campus, leaving Antony with the lion's share of the school's administration. However, the rift between the two men related to certain of Stanley's activities which Antony believed were incompatible with the position that he held.

While Antony maintains that he never expected to be promoted to the principal's post on Stanley's demise, it would be entirely out of character for him not to have wanted the position. However, he wasn't in the running, and Edward Stanley was eventually replaced by Duncan (Bill) Ross.

Ross had a wide experience of British theatre. He had been an actor with the London Old Vic Company and had been the leader of the Young Vic Company for three years. He was most recently the manager of the Playhouse Theatre in Nottingham. He is said by some of his Bristol colleagues to have been, 'a vital and energetic teacher', 'wise and gifted', with a dynamic persona, forthright views, and hair, variously described as 'unruly red-blond' or 'glowing ginger'.* He was also very lucky in that he took over the school at a time when it was soon to move from its dingy beginnings above the fruit and veg warehouse into a pair of magnificent Victorian villas that it still occupies today. One of Antony's students by the name of Julian Slade had made that move possible.

Slade had enrolled in the school in 1951, but had failed to make the grade at the end of his first year. Nevertheless, he was clearly a talented musician and composer and Antony persuaded the head of the BOV Company to take him on as a musical director. In 1954 Slade wrote the score for *Salad Days,* a musical which ran for over two thousand performances in London's West End and generated sufficient royalties to make the purchase of the 'new' BOVTS buildings possible.

*Bristol Old Vic Theatre School *the first 50 years 1946 – 1996.* by Shirley Brown

The new school, with Duncan Ross at its head, was opened by Dame Sybil Thorndike on June 26, 1956. However, by this time Antony had become jaded with both the school and with British theatre in general and was looking for a complete change of lifestyle.

In early 1957 Antony and his family would leave England for the Lower Mainland of British Columbia where they planned to purchase some land and become market gardeners. Before he left, Antony had a farewell drink with actor Peter O'Toole in the Duke's Head Pub near the Theatre Royal, Bristol.

O'Toole couldn't understand why Antony would give up everything and start over in a foreign country. This surprised Antony as the swashbuckling actor had a reputation for being adventurous – especially with young women. It had been a particular issue for Antony who had been so worried about the possible fallout should any of his impressionable young female students fall into bed with O'Toole that whenever he discovered that the actor was drinking in a particular pub he would put it out of bounds.

Antony's days as one of the prime movers behind the Bristol Old Vic Theatre School were over, but his legacy lives on, and, after sixty five years of existence, the alumni of the BOVTS is a *Who's-Who* of world theatre and film: Simon Cadell, Daniel Day-Lewis, Jeremy Irons, Jane Lapotaire, Phyllida Law, Pete Postlethwaite, Norman Rossington, Peter Baldwin, Christopher Gaze, Kenneth Cope, Gene Wilder and Sophie Thompson – to name just a few.

**Antony, (leaning against tree), with his parents and brothers, Kaye and Kenneth.
Preparing to leave for Canada in 1957**

Act 12

The Bumpy Road to Stardom

Well, honour is the subject of my story.
I cannot tell what you and other men
Think of this life; but, for my single self,
I had as lief not be as live to be
In awe of such a thing as I myself.

(*Shak. Julius Caesar*)

The difference between stardom and total obscurity can be as illusive as will-o'-the-wisp. However, great success in any field nearly always stems from years of dedication coupled with a combination of support, opportunities, connections and good timing – being in the right place at the right time. Three of Antony's contemporaries – Laurence Olivier, John Gielgud and Alec Guinness – all came from moderately wealthy families; were educated at private schools and universities; were well connected with either luminaries or patrons of the theatre; and had established their careers just before the outbreak of the Second World War.

Antony's achievements, on the other hand, had been entirely of his own making, although the odds had always been against him. Without family support, higher education and social connections, Antony had relied entirely on his talent and timing. Antony's acting talent was unquestionable, but the war had curtailed his training at Labour Stage and changed the landscape of British theatre, thereby throwing his timing off. While he may have been very successful in Egypt, the 'right place' to get noticed was, and still is, London's West End and so, by the age of

103

thirty seven with a slew of young talent hitting the already overcrowded British stage, he was beginning to realize that he had missed the boat.

The grass is always greener… and the grass in temperate British Columbia is certainly some of the greenest in Canada, but Antony's choice of this particular Province had more to do with connections and opportunities than the landscape. The Canadian government was encouraging immigration in the late fifties and Antony had two uncles living in BC's Lower Mainland. He had also taught a number of Canadian students in Bristol who had constantly sung praises about their 'land of milk and maple syrup'.

And so, with dreams of escaping the theatre altogether and growing vegetables for a living, Antony and family sold their house in Frithville Gardens, London, and flew to Vancouver.

Unfortunately, things didn't work out: the Chinese had already sewn up the vegetable growing business in BC and suitable land was pricey. Canada was much more expensive than Antony had anticipated and money from the London house, which was intended to provide funds for at least a year, lasted only a few months.

Antony still believes that he and his family benefited from a richer life in Canada than if they had stayed in Bristol, but life was very difficult at first. He was given some work in radio drama by the CBC* at their studios in the Hotel Vancouver, but money was quickly running out. Gusta took a job stoning peaches on a night shift and then worked as a credit counselor at the Hudson Bay Company. Unfortunately, she had no knowledge of Canadian credit and was quite happy to accede to everyone's request, and she only lasted a week.

In desperation, Antony became a taxi driver in New Westminster and took an apartment in a neighbourhood plagued by inebriates and undesirables. He soon moved the family to Port Moody and rented a house for $100 a month, but after a few weeks received an eviction notice because the landlord hadn't paid the mortgage. Then Antony went to prison and everything stabilized.

In September of 1957 The Haney Correctional Institute (HCI) – a penal complex for men between sixteen and twenty three years – was opened. It was for young men convicted of non-violent offences such as car theft, fraud and break and enter. Selected prisoners were those who were believed most likely to benefit from an environment as similar to the

---

* The Canadian Broadcasting Corporation

community at large as possible; where inmates had jobs and were responsible for getting up and reporting for work on time. The inmates were called 'trainees' and were given educational and vocational training in addition to work experience in state of the art workshops.

The philosophy of the Haney Correctional Institute was based on the research of Dr. Coral Topping,[*] who argued in 1927 that the policy of locking prisoners up and throwing away the key was not working. Prisons were failing both the prisoners and the populace at large because released offenders were almost certain to end up committing crimes and returning to jail.

Topping advocated changes to the system that would include, among others: segregation of young prisoners from long-term hardened offenders; maintenance of family and community ties; and provision of educational, vocational and recreational programs. Although Topping's views were widely supported at the time it took thirty years for any to be implemented, and then only on a trial basis at Haney.

David Barrett, who later became Premier of British Columbia, was head of the socialization program at HCI and said at the time that the idea was to prepare a trainee for a responsible life, adding, "We feel that letting trainees associate with members of the community gives them a better opportunity to effect their transition in society".

Some trainees participated in boxing tournaments in the community, and the basketball team played in the local league, but Barrett wanted to introduce some more cultural activities into the program so he advertised for an experienced drama teacher. John Braithwaite, who was soon to take over as Warden at the institute, says that Barrett couldn't believe his luck when he got the ex-Assistant Principal of Bristol Old Vic Theatre School to run the program.

However it was also a lucky day for Antony. With fewer unsavoury characters and no drunks to deal with, being in prison was better than cab driving in New Westminster. One slight snag was that Barrett had no budget approval for a drama teacher, but he did have money for an assistant librarian. So Antony started off by doing play readings in the library, which no one queried.

Just when everything seemed to be going well, the house Antony was renting was sold from under him and the new owners showed up

[*]Dr. Coral Topping: Governor of Kingston Jail, Ontario 1917 – 1919 and professor of sociology at University of British Columbia 1929 – 1954.

with their furniture. However, a nearby house with a half-acre lot was for sale and a trainee who had been a real estate agent, until he was busted for some dodgy dealing, explained how Antony could buy the property with just $100 deposit. The place cost $8,000 – a fortune, but it was better than being constantly evicted.

Antony's play reading group got off to a slow start, but when he said, "Let's put on a Christmas show", he had plenty of volunteers. The variety show was only for the entertainment of other inmates but Antony had bigger things in mind and, as 1958 unfolded, Antony introduced his group of play readers to a wider audience in the local community and arranged for drama groups to visit the institute and perform their readings. By the fall of that year Antony and his group were ready to take the leap into a full-scale stage production.

Antony first suggested his signature piece, Williams' *Night Must Fall*, but John Braithwaite didn't want trainees getting ideas from Danny; the charming young psychopathic murderer. In any case, the chosen play could have no women characters as the Warden's immutable rule was that no trainee was to play a female role. The play also had to include as many parts for trainees as possible to keep their interest. However, finding plays with a large all-male cast was difficult.

Antony eventually settled on Bevan and Trzcinski's play *Stalag 17*, a fitting though slightly ironical choice in that it is about a group of prisoners. But the trainees were all keen to act, including one particularly rebellious young man who had been a big troublemaker and was often in The Hole – a solitary confinement punishment cell with no furniture and just a hole in the floor for a toilet. Antony cast him in a major role and his behaviour improved dramatically overnight.

The play was a smash hit in January of 1959 with an audience of over 500 in the institute's own theatre, and critic, Janet Guppy, wrote, "It proved to the outside world that the men who live within the walls of a correctional institute may contribute something worthwhile to artistic life in our society". John Braithwaite, the young Chief Warder, had invited senior police officers, judges and other dignitaries to see the play. Vancouver radio talk show host, Jack Webster, Vancouver Sun columnist, Jack Wasserman, and George Archer the Chief Constable of Vancouver, all attended that show, and subsequent shows, at Haney and they all went off without a hitch, (other than the Chief Constable accidentally locking his keys in his car while attending one performance. But he was in luck; there were plenty of skilled car thieves in the cast and plenty of wire coat hangers in the wardrobe).

The show's success was a huge feather in the cap of the Warden, John Braithwaite, and Newsweek Magazine would eventually publish an article about the progressive rehabilitation program. The performance was seen as marking a milestone in the attitude of British Columbians toward prisoners, but, as Braithwaite and Antony would eventually discover, it was just a mile too far for many conservative Canadians. The programs for the play included the notation, "By kind permission of the Director of Corrections for British Columbia". However, this inscription would later cause something of an embarrassment to the Director when, perhaps predictably, the 'lock 'em up and throw away the key' brigade eventually bayed for blood.

However, in April of 1959 Antony was on a roll. Never having been a man to do things by half, he entered the first act of *Stalag 17* in the BC Drama Association's 10th. One-Act Play Festival in Vancouver. It was a potentially risky move. The spotlight would be on the prisoners; one escape attempt or a single incident of theft or bad behaviour would doom the whole experiment. It was also a bold move. Antony's troupe of miscreants would be competing against ten of the best amateur dramatic groups in the Greater Vancouver Area. On the other hand, any degree of success would be a complete vindication of the institute's raison-d'être.

And so, on Thursday, April 30, 1959, the Haney Correctional Institute became the first penal institution in North America to present a play to the general public outside of its own establishment...and they won!

The HCI Drama Group actually garnered three awards: The 2nd. Best Production, the Award of Merit for acting by the trainee who played the part of Hoffy,* and, especially gratifying for Antony, the award for The Best Director.

Following the trainees' success, and the very positive publicity it garnered for the institute, John Braithwaite was eager to extend the program. But Antony needed actresses if he was to do more plays, and he turned to the community for help with his next production, *Harvey*.

The Alouette Players were a local amateur theatrical company founded by Audrey Sumner, the English wife of a Haney doctor. Audrey

*Note ...In order to protect the guilty, trainees' names were never divulged or published in HCI presentations.

had been involved in amateur dramatics in the U.K. for many years and when she and her husband immigrated to Canada she had formed the group: first for play readings and later for performances in an abandoned church which she had turned into a theatre – complete with a bar.

A number of the Alouettes acted in plays with the trainees, although rehearsals at the institute were sometimes hampered by the regulations, especially the constant locking and relocking of doors. However there were no problems with the trainees who were always very polite and treated the women with great respect.

Many local women got their first view of the inside of a prison when they acted with Antony's group, and Audrey appeared as Mrs. Chauvenet in Mary Chase's *Harvey*, and later in their production of George Kaufman's, *You Can't Take It With You*, as Olga, a struggling duchess.

The leading character in *You Can't Take It With You* is a wealthy capitalist and the trainee playing the part needed a dinner suit for the role. The trainee actually owned a tuxedo but had left it in a motel when he was on the run, so Antony quietly retrieved it for him. However, the institute's psychologist objected to this particular trainee playing this role because it reinforced his delusion that he was a big shot. Antony prevailed and the resultant show was another success for the troupe.

The next play by Antony's group of trainees was Bella and Samuel Spewack's, *Boy Meets Girl*, produced in December of 1960, again with members of the Alouette Players, and the CBC's reviewer commented that it was so funny that the actors were fighting against the chaos in the audience.

The wardrobe mistress for this play was Antony's wife and a note in the program reads that Gusta took the job in order to "see her husband", adding her somewhat acerbic comment, "…if you can't beat 'em, join 'em". Antony's dedication to his craft was obviously interfering with his family life – a perennial complaint.

By early 1961, the Haney Correctional Institute Drama Group had played to audiences totaling in excess of 14,000 when they presented Antony's satirized adaptation of Mary Braddon's, *Lady Audley's Secret*, to sold-out audiences at the Cambie Street Theatre in Vancouver…

Haney Correctional Institute
British Columbia
February 1961

Dear Friend

Father always said that if I went on the stage I would probably end up in jail, and he was right. But, as I tell the inmates here, Cassius had the right idea in Julius Caesar when he said, *"Nor stony tower, nor walls of beaten brass, Nor airless dungeon, nor strong links of iron, Can be retentive to the strength of spirit;"*

We are doing Lady Audley's Secret, but I thought it was a bit dull so I changed a few things and somehow turned a melodrama into a rip-roaring comedy. For instance, Herbert Tree, the Victorian director, once used badgers, squirrels and a herd of deer to create the dawn scene in 'A Midsummer Night's Dream', so I thought, "Why not? If it was good enough for Tree..." So I got a couple of rabbits ... Don't laugh – it was the best I could do. Anyway, we had a full house and as the lights came up there were the cute little bunnies, mid-stage, in the glare of the morning sun – humping as only rabbits can hump. The audience loved it and giggled all the way through the first act. The play was a huge success and the theatre has held us over...this hasn't happened to me since Cairo.

By the way, I hear that Rudi Shelley has taken over my acting lessons at Bristol. I should be careful what I write in my letters – one day they will get me into trouble – but Shelley...teaching acting! [*]

Antony

[*]Although Shelley was a very popular teacher at BOVTS for many years he had no experience or background in acting and Antony was very surprised that he had been given the post.

Apart from ten year old Antony's Sunday school play, *Inspector Trent's Last Case*, his only theatrical penmanship had involved rewriting the works of others, including Shakespeare, in order to 'improve' them, give himself a larger role, or make them fit the cast available. While his efforts have not always been appreciated by purists, his satirization of *Lady Audley's Secret* was clearly brilliant. Even without the sexual antics of a couple of rabbits the play was apparently hilarious, and Desmond Arthur of the Vancouver Sun wrote, "*Lady Audley's Secret* is the brightest, cleverest show I've seen this season. I look forward to seeing future productions under Mr. Holland's inspired direction".

The first show at The Cambie Theatre was such a huge success that the Warden wanted more (performances, not humping bunnies), so Antony entered the first act of this play, featuring only one rabbit, into the 12th. Greater Vancouver One-Act Festival at the York Theatre in April of that year.

The competition was stiff: the top thirteen amateur theatrical groups from the area vying for recognition as the best in Vancouver together with a ticket to the provincial finals in Victoria.

Without the rabbits there was no distraction and Antony's troupe performed flawlessly. The adjudicator described the presentation as "an unusually brilliant piece of work by a competent team of actors", and, according to one reviewer, "The audience was most disappointed, not by the play, but because they only got to see the first act".

However, Antony had not been content with directing his own group in the festival. Much to his wife's disapproval he had also taken a leading role in the Alouette Players presentation of Terrance Rattigan's *The Browning Version*. And, while the adjudicator was fairly unenthusiastic about the Alouette's performance in general, she singled Antony out for praise; congratulating him on his complete mastery of the part.

With such glowing critiques from the adjudicator it wasn't a complete surprise that *Lady Audley's Secret*, by the Haney Correctional Institute's Drama Group, won the top award in the competition, or that Antony was lionized as the 'Best Actor' for his performance in *The Browning Version*. However, there was some murmuring in the Vancouver press about a professional actor and director masquerading as an amateur.

Nevertheless, Antony and his players had won, and their success had caught the attention of the public. Their performance was rated by one reviewer as "the funniest show to hit Vancouver for years".

Antony was justifiably proud of their achievement and in one interview with a reporter said that he had been trying for three years to convince people that amateur theatricals were an important facet of the program of an institute that is part of the penal system. However, not everyone was happy with the result of the competition, including an anonymous armchair critic who wrote to the press under the nom-de-plume, 'Theatre Minded', complaining that the adjudicator had indulged her passion for 'low comedy' and claiming that the first act of a three-act play did not constitute a one-act play and was therefore ineligible for the competition.

Despite the criticism, the Haney players had been declared the winners and were invited to represent Greater Vancouver in the British Columbia One-Act Play Festival in Victoria at the end of May. However, a constant problem that Antony faced was the transient nature of his actors and crew. When casting a play, a director's first question is usually, "Can he act?" But at Haney, Antony's first question had to be, "How long is he in for?" Two of the best actors were released from the institute during the run of *Lady Audley's Secret,* and had to be replaced, while the stage manager was paroled just a week before the big competition in Victoria and had to apply for permission to go back inside for rehearsals etc. The Warden eventually agreed that the parolee could participate, on condition that he signed a long list of promises: not to bring in drink, drugs, or take out letters or messages. He agreed but nothing in the document said he couldn't go out of the institute drunk. His fellow prisoners had made a batch of hooch to celebrate their success and he had partaken – fully.

Act 13

Antony Holland - Victoria Rex!

There is a tide in the affairs of men,
Which, taken at the flood, leads on to fortune;
Omitted, all the voyage of their life
Is bound in shallows and in miseries.
On such a full sea are we now afloat;
And we must take the current when it serves,
Or lose our ventures.

(Shak. *Julius Caesar*)

Saturday, June 3, 1961, and the eyes of Canadians were upon the City of Victoria on Vancouver Island where a group of convicted criminals were preparing to take to the stage to compete against the cream of British Columbia's amateur thespians.

This was the stuff of movies: *The Longest Yard; The Mighty Ducks; Greenfingers*, and at this point it would make an exciting and, for some, more believable narrative to relate how a few of Antony's young villains used their costumes and props to escape, took sexual liberties with the actresses backstage or plundered the theatre's box office, but nothing could be further from the truth. Warden John Braithwaite reports that there was not a single adverse incident involving the trainees in all of their off-campus performances.

However, there was a great deal of head scratching over transportation and housing of the trainees (and whether they should be allowed to perform at all) in the offices of the Directorate of Corrections and the Attorney General. When the drama program was introduced at Haney no one in the administration could have imagined that in just three years their wards would be on the cusp of being proclaimed the Province's top amateur actors. But they had reckoned without Antony Holland – a consummate headline grabber. Here was a man who at the age of sixteen had produced shows with posters and programs pretentiously headlined, 'A.E.Holland Presents...'; a man who, as an eighteen year old newspaper critic, had berated amateur actors for their amateurism; a man who, as a twenty one year old private soldier in Egypt, had propelled himself and a bunch of his mates into the limelight at one of the world's most prestigious theatres. And so it was probably inevitable that he would eventually find a way to break the inmates out of the obscurity of the correctional institute and into the public eye.

Nine amateur theatrical groups from as far afield as Campbell River, Kamloops and Kitimat had qualified to represent their respective regions in the 9th. Annual British Columbia Drama Festival in Victoria, and the competition was tough.

Mrs. Florence James, the adjudicator from Regina, was described in the Vancouver Sun as, "An International Drama Authority", although more than one critic questioned her credentials following her evaluation of some of the performances. However, when it came to her critique of the Haney group's Lady Audley's Secret, no one disagreed. She called it a memorable experience in theatre, saying, "You don't often see anything so right". She then went on to say that it was an admirable performance and that she couldn't remember when she had seen anything done so well. Jack Richards, theatre critic for the Vancouver Sun, wrote that Mrs. James was not alone in her praise, and that the entire house had roared their approval at the side-splitter and all had wanted to see more.

The adjudicator loved it; the press loved it; the audience loved it...and even the Provincial Attorney-General, Robert Bonner, attended the performance and gleefully described it as "Marvelous". And so it wasn't a major surprise when Florence James took to the stage and announced that not only had the production won the top prize but that she was awarding every cast member a special certificate of merit for their acting.

The trainees of the model correctional institution at Haney had won the biggest prize for amateur theatre in Western Canada, and the headline in the following morning's Daily Colonist was, "Prison Therapy

Wins Drama Festival". Congratulations poured onto John Braithwaite's desk but there was a cloud looming on the horizon: the idea that prisoners were going to jail for a joyride had conservatives up in arms and it wouldn't be long before the knives came out for the program at Haney.

It was the beginning of the end for Antony. Before his stunning success in Victoria he had applied to be recognized and paid as a drama therapist as opposed to an assistant librarian, but nothing had changed. Consequently, when The John Howard society had offered him a job as a social worker he had taken it. Warden John Braithwaite was well aware of the beneficial effects of Antony's program at Haney, not to mention the positive publicity, and hadn't wanted to lose him, so he had persuaded him to carry on directing plays part-time at almost the same wages as before – an arrangement that was to last for several years.

Photo - Anon

1961 Antony wins, "Best Director" trophy.

The John Howard Society is an organization for the rehabilitation of people released from government institutions and Antony already had connections with them. David Barrett, one of Antony's greatest supporters at Haney, was now with the society, having lost his job at the correctional institute when he ousted the incumbent labour minister, Lyle Wicks, in a provincial election.

Antony had no qualifications or experience as a social worker, but the Vancouver branch of the society was convinced that drama therapy was all that many of their clients needed in order to stay out of trouble. And so Antony did what he had always done – he formed a theatrical group. 'The John Howard Players' was composed of staff, semi-professional actors and clients, including some serious criminals. At the Haney Correctional Institute Antony always faced the possibility that his actors would be released before their performance, but now he had the opposite problem, and in one play, Elmer Rice's *The Adding Machine*, one of the cast members, an ex-prisoner, took off to Florida with a stolen cheque writing machine. He was caught and landed back in jail.

Antony's boss at the time was Peter Stein. He had a family of five children and they all became friends with Antony's family, and one day Antony revealed that he and his family were naturists and suggested they should all go together to The Surrey Sun Club – a nudist camp. After the initial surprise had worn off, Peter and his family went and he now says that it was a life altering experience. Antony's daughter, Rosheen, comments on the family's experience with nudism, saying, "We became naturists and I'm very grateful and blessed that we had a free and broad experience; culturally and morally – certainly not religiously."

Although Antony continued directing plays at Haney while he was with The John Howard Society, and later at Vancouver City College, the trainees would never again find themselves in the full glare of the public spotlight. However, in 1966 Antony did stage a performance of *Naked Island*, a play based on the novel by Russell Braddon, with the Haney group at Simon Fraser University (SFU) in Vancouver. Michael Bawtree, an English playwright and dramaturge, was the First Resident in Theatre at SFU at the time and he collaborated with Antony in staging the play. The performance attracted a large audience and was well received, but Michael's overarching memory is of the armed guards standing at each of the doors to prevent escapes.

Intense political pressure on S. Roxborough-Smith, the Director of Corrections, eventually caused him to pull the plug on performances of the drama group outside of the institute. This political pressure may also have been in response to Antony entering the political arena and running as a candidate for the opposition, the New Democratic Party, in the riding of Vancouver, Point Grey.

It has been more than eighty years since Dr. Coral Topping expressed his progressive views on incarceration, and fifty years since the Haney Drama Group won the coveted provincial One-Act Play Drama Festival, but little has changed in the penal system. John Braithwaite, the Warden at Haney in Antony's day, says that it was a good experience and that Antony made a great contribution to the establishment and to the individuals involved in his program, but that the concept of treating prisoners as worthwhile members of society who shouldn't be simply caged still represents a challenge to politicians and the community as a whole.

The Many Faces of Antony Holland

Portrait of Antony - 2009

By kind permission of Jean Paul photography, Desparats, Ontario.

The Many Faces of Antony Holland

Table of Contents

Plate 1

Plate 2

Plate 3

Plate 4

Plate 5

Plate 6

Plate 7

Plate 8

Plate 9

Plate 10

Act 14

Love's Labour's Lost

When you shall these unlucky deeds relate,
Speak of me as I am; nothing extenuate,
Nor set down aught in malice: then must you speak
Of one that loved not wisely but too well;
Of one not easily jealous, but being wrought
Perplex'd in the extreme; of one whose hand,
Like the base Indian, threw a pearl away
Richer than all his tribe:

(Shak. Othello)

Antony Holland is an archetypal self-starter who has rarely stepped into other men's shoes. Over and over again he has started from scratch: found the venue; cast the performers; molded the script to his liking; rehearsed relentlessly; and, finally, wowed the audience with his performance. And then he has moved on to another gig. He has directed each chapter of his life as if it was his next play, and such was the case when a brand new college in Vancouver advertised for an instructor to set up and head their theatre-arts program.

The Vancouver City College (VCC), which was later segregated into The Vancouver Community College and Langara College, was founded in 1965 as a vocational training institute for students seeking a practical education in fields such as journalism, photography, catering and theatre-arts, and in the fall of that year Antony took to the podium at the college's King Edward campus to teach his first acting class.

Antony is proud of his achievements as a non-academic in a sphere dominated by university graduates and, while his more modest schooling may not have always served him well, his knowledge, skill and accomplishments far surpass those of many of his better educated peers.

Today, Langara College's 'Studio 58' theatre-arts course, which grew from Antony's program, is ranked as one of the best, and is one of the most sought after, in Canada, but on Tuesday, September 7, 1965 Antony was the sole teacher and had just five students, four of whom were, in his words, "complete duds."

The original program at VCC had been devised by intellectuals before Antony's appointment and included psychology, business administration, physical education and English, with two periods of acting each week. While his workload would have been easy teaching just two afternoons a week, Antony knew from his experience in Bristol that a worthwhile theatre program needed to be almost entirely practical and had to include movement, dancing, singing, fencing, make-up and stage management in addition to acting, and he soon had the curriculum changed. However, he couldn't change the students. Only one of his greenhorns, an attractive young woman, had any acting acumen, so he started evening classes to fill the program and put the course on the map. He soon had thirty part-time students to supplement his corps of available talent and was able to plan his first production.

In Charles Dyer's *Rattle of a Simple Man,* a naïve youth from the countryside is goaded by his mates into spending time with a prostitute – in many ways reflecting Antony's own experience as a virgin soldier in Cairo (and with a similar dissatisfactory outcome).

The script called for the actress playing the prostitute to simply take off her dress – nothing else – but when the Vice Principal walked in on a rehearsal he ran straight to the Principal and had the play banned. This was in the mid sixties when nudity in the theatre on Broadway and London's West End was no longer novel, nor obscene, but the sight of a girl without a dress on the stage in Vancouver was still enough to bring out the smelling salts. Nevertheless, once the heads of the drama programs at the Universities of British Columbia and Simon Fraser had been summoned and had given it a clean bill of health, the play went on, and the girl's dress came off.

Antony accepted all-comers to his theatre-arts program at first, just to fill the seats, and he had a much larger group in the second year, including some talented students. He was soon able to give up the evening classes but he was still working part-time at the Haney Correctional Institute and was also directing plays for a number of community theatres. At one time he had four plays in production simultaneously and was, as usual, spending little time at home with his family.

Nevertheless, with a plethora of capable and committed students at Vancouver City College, Antony was soon eyeing the possibility of making more work for himself by producing a fully staged production. However, the facilities allotted to him in the old King Edward High School building were as inadequate as those he had encountered when he started at the Bristol Old Vic School – just a single large room with chairs and a piano – although, unlike the smelly room above the fruit and veg merchant's in Bristol, his classroom in Vancouver was in an airless, windowless basement.

The Broadway hit musical *Oh What a Lovely War* (a scathing socio-political examination of the First World War by Joan Littlewood's Theatre Workshop) was Antony's choice for his first show, and Michael Bawtree at Simon Fraser University agreed to loan his theatre for the performance. All Antony needed to complete his ensemble was a military style band, and the music department head at the college was happy to volunteer his students' services.

Antony rehearsed his actors and singers with a pianist, while the band practiced separately, and in a nod to Stanislavski he enlisted a regular army sergeant major to drill the cast members into a soldierly squad. For marching practice, the students paraded around the college neighbourhood in full military uniform during their lunch hours. It was good for publicity, but it wasn't appreciated by an officious inexperienced young police officer ...

King Edward Campus
Vancouver City College
May 1967

Dear Friend

I thought there were some boneheads in my class until I met the local cop. He saw my lads in uniform practicing for 'a Lovely War' and arrested them for belonging to a mercenary army – Imagine ... Antony Holland's Brigade of weak-kneed Thespians! Hah! I tried explaining, but he just kept saying, "Membership of a private army is illegal in Canada, Sir."

"There are more things in heaven and earth, Constable, than are dreamt of in your philosophy." I said, but he looked puzzled. "They're just actors." I protested, "Any fool can see that – Just look at them." That stopped him, but not for long. "They look like a private army to me, Sir. So I'll let the law decide."

"Repair thy wit, good youth, or it will fall to cureless ruin," I warned him, reminded of Shylock's court scene in the Merchant. *"I stand here for the law."*
But whichever kindergarten he'd just graduated from obviously didn't teach Shakespeare.

He left, red-faced, once the Principal phoned his Inspector, but the fun wasn't over. I got the students to dig a trench in the grounds, World War I fashion, and made them live in it for a few days – shades of Stanislavski...(though he would have sent them to the East German border for a year or two). Then it rained. "Realism," I said, as if I'd planned it, but they were sloshing about in mud up to their knees, so I gave them a tent and I let them march about the grounds and keep guard just like I had done in Llandudno at the start of the war.

The next thing: the psychiatric patients in the hospital next door spotted the boys, thought they were under attack, and freaked out. What fun!

Antony

Helen Volkow was a student in Antony's program at the time and recalls that the nurses on the psychiatric ward at Vancouver General Hospital eventually sedated their patients; checked out their claims; realized what was happening; and wrote a funny letter addressed to, "The boys at the front", but for Helen the most poignant moment of the staging of *Oh What a Lovely War* was the eighty year old WW1 stretcher bearer Antony enlisted to speak to the students during rehearsals. Helen was just nineteen years old at the time and from that day on has understood the dreadful consequences of war.

Apart from the slight contretemps with the police and the disturbance at the hospital, all was going well with the production until the head of the music department dropped a bombshell by demanding three thousand dollars to pay the musicians. Antony was outraged and had no intention of paying students – but they weren't students. The music teacher had been too embarrassed to admit that most of his students weren't up to the task so had hired some professionals to make them sound good, and the pros had to be paid union rates.

The show was advertised, and Antony's students had put their hearts (and their feet) into it, so the Principal eventually agreed to pay. But, in an effort to prove his worth, the music teacher had gone overboard and a full twelve piece military band showed up at the dress rehearsal and completely drowned out the singers. Antony eventually reined in the band and the show was a great success.

Antony's continuing part-time work at the correctional institute gave some of his female students an opportunity to act with the inmates and Helen Volkow says that the best thing about going to Haney was that she and the other girls got to ride in Antony's Rolls-Royce Silver Cloud, although they had to sit on their hands so as not to put fingerprints on the highly polished mahogany trim.

Antony bought the Roller on a whim in 1967, thereby satisfying an aspiration which he had held since a young teenager in Tiverton when the sight of a Rolls-Royce had been even more tantalizing than Beryl Andrew's breasts. The chief mechanic at his father's garage had contributed to this yearning by his almost religious adulation of the marque, and he had overawed Antony by taking him on a test run of a customer's Rolls and demonstrating that he could drive it uphill in first gear and step out to stroll alongside while the car would gently purr along all by itself.

Antony's Rolls-Royce was his pride and joy and, because of his background and experience, he not only serviced the vehicle himself but was able to maintain it in award-winning condition. The pristine car won many awards, and opened a few very expensive doors in California – albeit at the homes of men who owned several of the prestigious cars – and one of Antony's saddest days was when he was eventually forced to sell it.

It would be many years before the car was sold, but the seeds of its destiny had been sown a few years earlier when Antony was working for the John Howard Society. He had been directing The John Howard Players in a play and one evening after rehearsal he had given a young actress a ride home and, in a scene straight out of a Woody Allen movie, she invited him in for coffee, went into her bedroom and came out stark naked.

Photo - Anon

Antony shows off his beloved Rolls-Royce

Antony's infidelity would eventually cost him his marriage – and his Rolls-Royce – and today he looks back at the affair with great regret and attributes his response to male menopause or midlife crisis: discounting the possibility that many men in their mid forties faced with a totally naked, attractive and very willing ingénue, might have done exactly the same as he. Whatever the reasoning, the deed was done and the relationship lasted for about nine months until the young woman flew off to be an airline stewardess in the States. And that could have been an end to the matter... had they not written to each other, and had Antony not kept the letters in a place where his wife would subsequently find them several years later.

By the time that Antony's marriage was falling apart, his program at the King Edward campus was coming together and he was able to expand into a newly acquired portable classroom, reminiscent of the wartime army huts he had occupied in Egypt. He was still struggling to recruit sufficient talented students and had yet to introduce auditions for applicants, although he would do his best to dissuade absolute no-hopers. One such applicant was Maysie Hoy. Maysie was from a strict traditional Chinese background where actresses were equated with hookers. Her family owned a restaurant in Vancouver and she was studying to be a dietician in the food services program (at her parents' instigation) until she saw how much fun Antony's students were having. Antony tried very hard to put her off, believing that there would be few opportunities in the business for a Chinese girl, but she was determined. "This is what I have always wanted to do", she told him and he eventually relented, but, she says, "He barely spoke to me for two years. He just left me alone to my own devices."

Maysie Hoy is now one of the most sought after film editors in Hollywood. She is on the Board of Directors in both the Motion Picture Editors Guild and American Cinema Editors and was featured in Helena Lumme's book, *Great Women of Film...* and Antony has never stopped apologizing to her for his lack of confidence and encouragement.

By the fifth year, when Antony's program was preparing to move into the new Langara Campus, the number of applications had risen to the point where it was necessary to hold auditions for places. Auditions are nerve-racking events for most actors in the best of circumstances, but Antony had developed ways to further ratchet up the pressure in order to weed out weak candidates.

Pru Olenik had travelled from Alberta for her audition and was surprised when Antony ushered her into his small, cluttered office on the blatant pretext that the stage was in use. Antony deliberately allowed the tension to rise in the confined space before telling her to begin her prepared piece, but then, after a minute or so, he yawned extravagantly, pulled out a newspaper and began reading – obscuring his face completely. Pru was determined not to be rattled and vainly searched for an appropriate moment in the scene to swat the newspaper out of his hands. Antony guffawed loudly at the end of her presentation, gave her a long, hard look, then smiled and offered her a place on his course. Pru was so angry that she glared back at Antony and told him to put it in writing.

Antony used this 'newspaper trick' over the years to disconcert many students and actors who had spent weeks or months learning a piece, and they would have no way of knowing what he thought of their performance, or even if he had fallen asleep (which he was prone to do on occasions), until he showed his disapproval with a 'snap' of the paper or he offered a well chosen comment at the end.

The new campus on West 49th. Avenue in Vancouver, which would become the home of Langara College's renowned Studio 58 (a name chosen by Antony simply because it was the room number) was on the drawing board in the late sixties and Antony was determined that he should get suitable accommodation for his theatre-arts department. Unfortunately, the President, Bert Wales, appeared more interested in car parking than theatre and at a meeting called to unveil the building plans proclaimed with great sincerity that the campus would have the most beautiful parking lot in all of Vancouver. Antony laughed, but the President persisted, saying, "No – Seriously. It's even going to have trees".

The eventual parking lot certainly had plenty of trees: seemingly at the expense of Antony's dream performance space which had somehow nightmare'd into another ugly basement room with no windows. Antony had been experimenting with plays without scenery, and with the actors changing costume in the round, and he wanted his performance space at Langara to be a simple pit surrounded by seating so that he could continue this style. He got the pit, but the planners hearing the words "theatre department" had reasoned that there had to be a stage, and if there was a stage then there should also be an enormous lighting booth from where the stage lights could be controlled. There was also a very awkwardly placed pillar and, worse, to the right of the stage was a massive grease trap that rumbled like a giant's empty belly whenever anyone washed the dishes in the cafeteria above and would occasionally overflow and rain greasy hot water onto the audience below.

Antony's disappointment didn't end with the stage and the enormous brick-built lighting booth. There was a large workshop adjacent to his room which Antony thought was his for producing props, and opposite was an unused room which he assumed he could use for movement classes. He was wrong on both counts. The workshop was not for props, and the empty room was allocated to the music department which was still at the King Edward campus. No amount of badgering would get the intransigent head of music to release the room and Antony was eventually forced to rent a room on Main Street for his movement classes.

The theatre-arts department may have been pushed to the bottom of the pile at Langara, but successful programs are founded on the commitment, knowledge and skill of the teachers and not simply the quality of the facilities. Under Antony's skillful mentorship Studio 58 would eventually rise from its basement beginnings to take centre stage in the world of Canadian theatre education.

Christopher Gaze now sits on the advisory committee of Studio 58 and says, "Good actors don't fall off trees and play Shakespeare, and Studio 58 is a precious resource. At least fifty percent of the cast of Bard on the Beach come from Studio 58 and we couldn't have achieved what we have without it."

By the time that Antony was preparing to move into his new accommodation at Langara College he had moved out of his marital home. Gusta had felt so betrayed by his infidelity that their marriage was over in all but name. Today, more than forty years later, Gusta acknowledges that she was terribly hurt by what had happened and she was later sickened by the sight of Antony driving around in his Rolls-Royce with young ladies in the seat beside him. She couldn't forgive him and admits that her opinions of Antony are still clouded by his unfaithfulness, while Antony admits that his biggest regret in life is that he destroyed his first marriage.

Act 15

To Sleep, Perchance to Dream

But, I pray you, let none of your people stir me:
I have an exposition of sleep come upon me.
(Shak: A Midsummer Night's Dream)

All theatrical directors have a preferred method of directing and, in his younger days, Antony's technique was to constantly leap onto the stage to demonstrate how a particular part should be played. This was a form of rote learning for the actors which didn't require them to analyze the character's motivations and display their inner thoughts; they just did what Antony told them to do. As Antony became more experienced he took a more arm's-length approach and, although he never totally embraced Stanislavski's system, he encouraged actors to discover their characters' objectives and to express their emotions without his continual guidance. This directing method allowed Antony to take a more relaxed role and Suzanna Ristic, playing the neurotic wife of a Nazi S.S. officer in C.P.Taylor's *Good* at Studio 58, says that Antony was so relaxed that he would direct from behind the daily newspaper and would sometimes fall asleep.

Antony was the Artistic Director of the theatre-arts program at Vancouver City College and Langara for twenty years and many of his students from that time recall him falling asleep while he was directing. However, Antony has also fallen asleep during actual performances and actor Dirk Van Stralen remembers appearing with him in 1999 when he fell asleep during the interrogation scene in Act II of *The Mouse Trap*.

Antony woke as the scene ended and just managed to leave the stage in time. Mike Mathews has a similar recollection: when Antony stretched out on a cot and fell deeply asleep during Mike's delivery of a lengthy monologue in a preview performance of Harold Pinter's, *The Caretaker*, at Malaspina College Theatre on Vancouver Island. Fellow actor, Tony Bancroft, realized that Antony was asleep as he made his next entrance and was able to wake him by getting close and raising his voice. The director, (Antony's second wife, Catherine), was not amused and made Antony sit upright throughout the speech in the following public performances.

While Antony's narcolepsy was an irritation to some, it was a source of amusement to others – especially when he fell asleep every night of a month-long run of a Christmas play at the Vancouver Playhouse. However, on one occasion it nearly proved fatal. Jonathon Bryden, a student at Langara in the mid seventies, recalls the time that Antony was directing him and fellow student Kerry Shale in their first play at Studio 58: John Wilson's *Hamp*. They had rehearsed the same piece several times and were waiting for criticism, or acclaim, when they saw that Antony was slumped in his director's chair with a newspaper across his chest. It wasn't unusual for Antony to sleep through rehearsals so they carried on until the door flew open and the stage manager rushed in with paramedics and carried him off to an ambulance. Rumours circulated that the students' acting had given Antony a heart attack, but he had actually collapsed with a hiatus hernia and the doctors wanted him admitted to hospital. Antony had other plans and explained that he was far too busy to be ill, so he signed himself out the same day.

Antony's relaxed persona, both on and off stage, belies the tremendous amount of sweat he has put into everything he has ever achieved. Nothing has come easily: he has no magic bullet; no photographic memory. He has simply poured all of his effort and his emotion onto the stage – sometimes to the detriment of his health and often to the detriment of his family life.

Lynna Goldhar had first hand experience of the depth of Antony's commitment to a role when she was a student at Studio 58, although she had met him previously when she was an eleven year old performing in a play directed by his first wife in Vancouver. Gusta had announced that the famous actor/director, Antony Holland, would watch their rehearsal and give notes, and young Lynna had badly wanted 'notes'. But, while Antony had critiqued others, he had said nothing to her, so she had eventually cornered him for his opinion. He had laughed and offered a few words of encouragement, and a decade later when she was in his class, pursuing her childhood dream to become an actress, she constantly worried that he might recognize her as the pushy eleven year old. In her second year at Studio 58 she was the ASM in a production of Brian Friel's tragicomedy *Philadelphia Here I Come*, in which Antony played a taciturn unaffectionate father, while her husband-to-be, Rob Smith, played Gareth, the son. In the play, Gareth is about to leave Ireland for America and is futilely seeking his father's affection over their last supper together. Antony had refused to speak directly to Rob throughout rehearsals to inject realism into their relationship and Rob was quite unnerved – as Antony intended. For the dress rehearsal, Lynna had searched high and low for the 'right' Irish meat pie demanded by Antony and finally got a 'note' from him, saying, "Wonderful pie. Let's have that every night for the run". And then, without making eye contact with Rob, he very coldly instructed Lynna to advise his 'son' that he was eating with his fork in the wrong hand.

Neither Lynna nor Rob knew of Antony's wounded relationships with both his father and with his own son that were reflected in this piece of theatre, but Antony's personal ghosts were clearly near the surface at times.

Nick Rice is another actor who has firsthand experience of the deep emotional side of Antony. In 1973 Nick was a student of theatre at the University of British Columbia and was playing Pedersen in Ibsen's *Wild Duck*. He recalls Antony, playing old Ekdal, as a quiet man who sat by himself reading the newspaper until his cue, when he would slowly get up, wander onstage, quietly say his lines, and then wander off: no pyrotechnics; no tragedian's voice; no physical tics; and not a drop of sweat. Just simple, unaffected, and real. "There must have been art," explains Nick, "Yet it was an art that concealed art."

Three years later Nick was invited to be part of the Westcoast Actors' production of *Merchant of Venice* for the CBC, directed by the famous English director, John Sichel. Nick was cast as Shylock's assistant, Tubal, with Antony playing the old Jew. "I couldn't imagine how such an un-actorish actor could play such a big part," says Nick, "But he didn't act. He simply was Shylock – a real human being who, like all human beings, doesn't know what he's going to say before he says it. He was not larger than life – he just *was* life. And the feelings he connected with were real. Before the scene where Shylock learns his daughter has fled with his ducats, Antony would slip away to a quiet room, or his van parked outside the stage-door, and I would find him quietly crying by himself. I don't know what his prep consisted of; what thoughts, images and memories he dredged up, but I would gently steer him to the wings and, just as he'd done in *Wild Duck,* he would simply wander onstage and play the scene brilliantly. Spencer Tracy once said, "Sure, go ahead and act. But don't ever let anyone catch you at it". I stood literally inches away from Antony Holland each night and if anyone could have caught him acting, it would have been me. I never did."

In the more than eighty years that Antony has been performing, directing and teaching, he has touched the lives of thousands of students and actors, hundreds of thousands of theatergoers, and countless millions who've watched him in movies and on television. And among these multitudes are many individuals whose lives have been radically changed by their encounter with him.

Jessie award-winning actress, Alana Shields, a graduate in 1977, commented on Antony in The Province newspaper at the time of his retirement in 1985. In words that could be echoed by thousands, she wrote, "What he did for me was to give me a really strong sense of value of what we do. He made me proud of that – it's something I'll always carry with me. And he instilled from very early on the importance of good work habits".

On Antony's eightieth birthday, Stephen Aberle recalled his first day at Studio 58 when Antony had told him and his cohorts that theatre was not therapy and that if they were there because their lives were a mess and needed sorting out they should please leave. However, Aberle went on to explain that, judging from the effect Antony had on so many lives, "I think it's fair to say he became a doctor in spite of himself".

Canadian Kerry Shale would concur with Stephen's assertion. He is an award-winning actor and voice artist who has one of the most recognizable voices on the BBC in Britain today. At twenty two Kerry was a drifter from Winnipeg with little ambition – a self-confessed pot-smoking hippie working as a parking lot attendant in Vancouver's drug-riddled Downtown East-side. His life was headed in the same direction as many of the addicted dropouts around him until he answered an advertisement for Studio 58. He had never envisaged becoming an actor and had little enthusiasm, but once he was accepted he was determined never to go back to the streets. Although, as he says, "It was a really tough course. Fail and you were out." Each term's highlight for Kerry was to perform a number of scenes for Antony, but these assessment sessions carried a risk. Antony was uncompromising and wouldn't hesitate to dismiss students who weren't excelling; of the twenty two who started with Kerry only six graduated. (Over the years approximately seventy five percent of all students failed the course).

Like many other students, Kerry's abiding memory of Antony is of his disconcerting trick of hiding, and sometimes sleeping, behind a newspaper during auditions and rehearsals, and he remembers well the day that Antony collapsed behind the paper while he and John Bryden were rehearsing, and he recalls praying, "Please don't let him die. This is my big break". After graduating, Kerry became a scholar of theatre history in London and to impress a girl he auditioned for a West End musical. To his amazement he got the role. He considered attending RADA or other famed U.K. academies but he just kept getting parts, and when he talked to fellow actors and directors he realized that it was because his training at Studio 58 was far superior to theirs at the Ivy League schools.

One of the reasons for the success of Studio 58 students was the real world experience they acquired from participating in a large number of full-scale productions. Antony was determined that students should be involved in as many productions as possible and under his twenty year leadership the college produced more than a hundred plays, but it was clear to him that a two-year program did not provide sufficient time to turn out fully proficient actors. Antony wanted to increase the length of the program to three years, but he faced a Ministry of Education ruling that required diploma courses to be completed in two. He wouldn't give up, especially when he discovered that Vancouver Community College had received a special dispensation from the Ministry to run a four-year art program on the grounds that it took that length of time to train an artist. Antony believed that the same argument should apply to his particular art form and wanted to similarly apply, but the administration at Langara College was opposed and he was emphatically told, "Yours is a two-year program – period".

Over the years many people have discovered the folly of turning Antony away: the crusty old-colonial running the amateur theatrical group in Cairo who ended up begging for tickets at the Royal Opera House; the major who refused to give him transport because all the troops wanted to see was musicals and large breasted women. So the administration at Langara might have been wise to accede to Antony's request. When Antony sets his mind to do something he will succeed if success is at all possible. Antony's daughter, Rosheen, knows this of her father and says, "I'm proud of him because of his ability to keep his focus. I give up if things get too tough, but he is courageous and honourable and when he decides to do something, he does it."

Antony's solution to the program length situation was simple: he would change the curriculum from two terms a year to three and work year round. Six terms over a two year period was effectively a three-year program and students who needed to take off summer terms could return in the third year, just like any student in any other course who missed, or was required to repeat, a term.

The three term year would be particularly hard on Antony but he was willing to suffer in order to give the students the education that he knew they would need, and the administration eventually relented and applied for special dispensation for a three-year acting program.

The vastly improved facilities at Langara (although not exactly to Antony's specifications) vis-à-vis the old King Edward campus enabled him to mount full-scale productions in his own performance space, and he decided to reprise *Oh What a Lovely War* for his first show in March 1971. However, the Principal and administration were against his choice because of its antiwar and antiestablishment theme. It was, perhaps, a reasonable concern at that time: there was growing antiwar sentiment against American operations in Southeast Asia leading to student strikes south of the border, and many students in Canadian universities were seeking an end to the conservative old-guard administrations and demanding democracy. Nevertheless, Antony dug in his heals, and went ahead with the production.

It is impossible to overstate the seriousness with which Antony views his craft. He is the ultimate professional in all things theatrical, and he doesn't take kindly to those who treat this 'world' disrespectfully. Helen Volkow, a student in 1966, still quakes at the memory of Antony tearing into her classmates for fooling around with the swords during a lunch break. And so his reaction was predictable when he discovered that the student 'soldiers' digging the trench and standing guard in preparation for this production of *O What a Lovely War* had filled their tent with young women and booze and turned their 'wartime' experience into a party, and he certainly wasn't happy with one of the girls in the cast who cut a performance because she, *'couldn't possibly miss a hockey game!'*

The critics were happier, although Antony admits that many of the plays he directed at Studio 58 received bad reviews. "They were just students," explains Antony in defense, "And I was always pushing the envelope and making them stretch."

Act 16

Reaching for the Stars

Be not afraid of greatness:
Some are born great,
Some achieve greatness,
And some have greatness thrust upon 'em.
(Shak. Twelfth Night)

In the late nineteen sixties the National Theatre of Great Britain performed at Vancouver's Queen Elizabeth Theatre, with Sir Laurence Olivier starring in George Feydeau's French farce, *A Flea in Her Ear,* and Congreve's *Love for Love,* and Robert Lang, a former student of Antony's from the Bristol Old Vic Theatre School, was in the cast with Olivier and arranged backstage passes for Antony and his students at Studio 58. Olivier, a man with extraordinary acting talent who worked extremely hard at his craft, had always been something of a role model for Antony, but he was incredibly egotistical and just had to better everyone else …

Vancouver
1969

Dear Friend

Can you believe it? We saw Olivier – in Vancouver!

Robert Lang slipped me past the doorman during tech rehearsal. "Sir Laurence …" I said with outstretched hand, but he was setting the stage and he blanked me out. "Sir Laurence …" I tried again, but now his eyes were up in the spotlights. He probably thought I was a hack from the local press or someone collecting for charity so I started again, "Sir …Sir…" It was no use; it was like trying to make eye contact with a nun in a nudist colony. Robert eventually came to my rescue and introduced me as his teacher, but Olivier was more interested in himself and the set than me.

At least we got tickets for the show – And what a hoot! Gusta and I were near the back but the Mayor and all the VIP's sat up front and tried to look intellectual. They obviously weren't because they spent too long in the bar at intermission, missed the bell, and couldn't get back to their seats for the second act. It was hilarious to see them lined up along the back wall in their finery like wallflowers at a dance.

Olivier thought they had skipped out on him and was so livid that he made a speech from the stage at the final curtain and addressed the empty front row as if it embodied the VIPs. "Mr. Mayor, Lady Mayoress, Madam Minister…" he started, bowing to each vacant chair in turn, and then he reeled off the entire cast of missing VIPs like a headmaster reading out a list of miscreants caught masturbating over Playboy behind the cycle shed.

The red-faced VIP's were whisked backstage for some 'splaining after the show, but Olivier's dresser stood guard and insisted that he was not there. They eventually left, heads down, and we found Larry sheepishly hiding out in Robert's dressing room.

Antony

P.S. I think it's OK to call him Larry now we're in on his little game – especially as he kissed Gusta.

Antony had another brush with British theatrical aristocracy a few years later when he was granted a second audience with Sir John Gielgud. Gielgud was performing Pinter's *No Man's Land* in London and Antony was hoping for some insight into the role, he was also hoping Gielgud had forgotten his stumble at their previous meeting in 1946. Gielgud didn't mention the stumble, but wasn't able to offer any useful advice either.

John Peter Sichel, an exalted British film and stage director, was to become yet another disappointment to Antony. He had directed Laurence Olivier and Joan Plowright in the award-winning movie of Anton Chekhov's *Three Sisters,* and in 1973 was head cameraman in a TV production of *The Merchant of Venice* starring Olivier. In 1976 Sichel was invited by the CBC to remount *The Merchant* for Canadian television, featuring Barney O'Sullivan and Micki Maunsell with Antony Holland in the role of Shylock. Antony hadn't played the part since 1947, but thirty years later he was able to walk in on the first day of the three day workshop without a script. It was rumoured among Studio 58 students that Antony could flawlessly recite the entire play (and had once done so in Egypt during the war to win a bet). True or not, Antony won a nomination for the ACTRA[*] 'Best Actor' award for his portrayal of Shylock, and Sichel was so impressed he presented Antony with the yarmulke that Olivier had worn in the British production.

Following the recording, Sichel suggested doing a Shakespeare series at Studio 58 and was contracted to direct *Romeo & Juliet, Othello* and *Hamlet.* Antony now admits that it was an awful mistake. Sichel turned out to be a megalomaniac when dealing with students and gave them a terrible time. He praised the bad ones and damned the good ones, and everyone suspected that he was having a fling with one of the young female students: a suspicion confirmed when he called the entire cast together and angrily declared, "I am not having an affair with her".

The CBC's production of *The Merchant* wasn't Antony's first foray onto the screen – although he was certainly a late bloomer as far as movie acting was concerned. His very first attempt had been as a judge in a 1967 television series titled *Caribou Country.* The episode, subtitled *How to Break a Quarter Horse,* starred First Nations leader, Chief Dan George, and is probably best left in the CBC vaults.

[*] The Alliance of Canadian Cinema, Television and Radio Artists

However, in 1971 came an opportunity that would launch Antony into a movie career that is still going strong forty years later. *McCabe & Mrs. Miller* is an American western, directed by Robert Altman, starring Warren Beatty and Julie Christie. In 2008 the American Film Institute judged the movie to be the eighth best film of all time in the western genre, while Julie Christie was nominated for an Academy Award for 'Best Actress' for her role as Mrs. Miller.

Antony had auditioned and got the usual, "Don't call us..." routine, but shooting had started without a call-back so he was surprised when his agent said that Altman wanted to see him. The director met Antony on the set – a nineteenth century mining town being filmed as it was being created on the outskirts of Vancouver – and the two chatted for awhile before Antony was introduced to Warren Beatty. Altman had made no mention of offering a part in the movie and so, after talking to Beatty about French films for awhile, Antony dejectedly headed to the parking lot. Moments later he was chased down by Altman's assistant and sent straight to wardrobe. He had got the part of a mining company's representative who wants to buy a mine from John McCabe (*Warren Beatty*), and Altman had even named the character, 'Ernie Hollander,' after him.

Maysie Hoy, the Chinese student whom Antony had tried so hard to discourage a few years earlier, played a prostitute in *McCabe and Mrs. Miller* and went on to appear in many Altman movies. Altman liked her and taught her all sides of the business – so much for Antony's assertion that there was no career path for Chinese people in theatre-arts.

On a personal front at the beginning of the seventies. Now that Antony was no longer with his first wife, although the divorce wasn't finalized until 1981, he had a number of relationships which he describes as 'insignificant'. Whether the women in question took the same cavalier view is unknown, but Jonathon Bryden recalls the gentle warning he received from Antony in 1976 when, as a student at Studio 58, he was attempting to bed every available actress in the school. "I tried to follow the advice," says Jonathon, "Even though it was coming from a Grand Thespian who was dating an aspiring actress at least twenty five years his junior."

Catherine Cains, who now uses her stage name of Kayte Summers, was twenty six years Antony's junior when she met him in February 1980. She was a thirty three year old undergrad student at the

University of British Columbia who was completing a four-year degree program and needed an equity actor to play a major role in her final project, a comedy called *Gas Works:* a play in which the leading actor portrays a number of different characters, including women.

Although Antony and Catherine would soon be a couple, she was overawed at their first meeting. "He was a legend," says Catherine, "He was the main man at Studio 58 and everyone was terrified of him." For his part, Antony recalls that he was concentrating on the script at the first rehearsal when he heard a familiar, and very distinct, Bristolian accent and his head shot up.

Age didn't matter to either: their British roots, connections to Bristol and love of the theatre were sufficient bases for an affair that would soon blossom into a marriage.

Catherine was an experienced actor and director specializing in anti-establishment plays dealing with social problems, so their leftwing ideologies meshed and they began working together on projects such as scenes from David French's *Creeps* which featured differently-abled actors.

By this time Catherine had begun an MBA program and needed off-campus experience, so Antony hired her to work at Studio 58 as an instructor and, in December 1981, they wed and became a team in every sense.

"He's a born romantic and he loves deeply," says Catherine thirty years later, "although people who love Antony can feel shut out because his work is everything. He's a consummate actor, but he overworks, overextends himself and would drop everything for a movie part."

Antony was in his sixties before he got into the movies and soon realized that movie making was considerably less stressful than the stage. He had known nothing about film acting until his first role in *How to Break a Quarter Horse* and didn't realize that the actors only kept up their character when actually on camera. While filming that episode he had played a judge and *was* the judge the whole time, but the other actors did their bit then relaxed with a coffee and brushed up their lines for their next speech while waiting for the camera to swing back their way.

As a distinguished-looking white male in the 1980s Antony was often typecast as a judge (something, he admits wryly, that no longer happens today because American judges are most often young black females). However, because of his professional ability to bond with his character's objectives, he would actually become a judge. For example: in *The Grey Fox,* a Canadian movie directed by Phillip Borsos, Antony thought the prison sentences he'd been given to hand out to the convicted felons were too lenient so he doubled them – and no one questioned it.

In 1982 Antony was a judge again, this time in an American movie directed by George Schaefer starring the legendary Bette Davis – Number 2 on the American Film Institute's list of the greatest female stars of all time behind Katharine Hepburn.

In *A Piano for Mrs. Cimino* Antony has three scenes with Bette Davis in which he has to determine whether or not her character, the aging Esther Cimino, is *compos mentis* and capable of taking care of her own affairs. Antony first met the Grande Dame of American cinema when Schaefer, who was known for his theatrical experience, called all the principals together for a full reading ...

Vancouver
1982

Dear Friend

My heart is still pounding so much I can hardly write!

George Schaefer got us assembled into a royal reception line and then Bette Davis swept in like a queen – the Queen of the Silver Screen. I couldn't believe it. I was ten when she made her first film and fifteen when she won her first Oscar, and there she was standing right in front of me asking my name. I felt as if I should bow.

We read till lunchtime and I rushed back afterwards to go over my lines again. Bette Davis was already there, alone, and we had a lovely chat. "You've done stage work. I can tell," she said, and then she told me about working with Ronald Reagan in the 1939 film *Dark Victory*.

"What was he like?" I said, and she pulled me close and whispered, "He wasn't a very good actor."

We finished the reading and started shooting and then, and this is the best bit, at the end of my third scene Bette Davis snatched the script from the assistant director's hand and stood behind the camera and fed me my lines. Everyone gasped; even Schaefer looked shocked – a Star feeding lines to a minor supporting actor!

And then, and this was truly unbelievable, when the assistant director called, "Thank you everybody. That's a wrap," Ms. Davis came out from behind the camera, walked across to me and turned to the crew. "Just a minute everybody," she said, "Before we wrap we should acknowledge the work of this very fine actor." And then she began applauding – all by herself. I was stunned and so were the crew. Bette Davis was clapping on her own for a couple of seconds and then they all joined in with loud applause. I think I want my epitaph to be... *Here lies an actor who was applauded by Bette Davis!*

Antony

A Piano for Mrs. Cimino was to be one of the last of more than a hundred movies starring Bette Davis. A year later she was diagnosed with breast cancer and, although she kept working till the end, she had a number of strokes and died in 1989. Her epitaph reads, "She did it the hard way", but it could have been, *"She applauded Antony Holland"*.

While Antony was again cast as a judge on this movie, he sometimes got parts that were a stretch. One movie called for an actor who could ride a horse and was good with guns. Antony couldn't ride and, despite his military training, wasn't a particularly good shot. He got the part anyway!

Antony has sometimes been confused with American movie actor Anthony Holland, who committed suicide in 1988, and several movies have incorrect credits as a result. One such movie is *The Best Christmas Pageant Ever* directed by George Schaefer in 1983. The movie stars Loretta Swit – best known as Major Margaret (*Hot-Lips*) Houlihan, the heartthrob the 4077th mobile medical unit in the long-running, and highly acclaimed, American television series, *M*A*S*H*. Antony has a key part in the movie as the Reverend Hopkins and has second-billing to Loretta Swit, (although the part is incorrectly credited to <u>Anthony</u> Holland, both on the movie itself and in the deceased actor's bio). However, despite the fact that Antony had watched episodes of *M*A*S*H*, he didn't recognize Swit during the filming. "I guess she was not so hot after all," says Antony, but he's grateful that he at least was paid for his work on this occasion.

In 1988 Antony made a low budget movie on the promise that he would receive payment if it made it at the box-office. He heard nothing and assumed that it had flopped, until several years later when another actor from the movie enthused about the royalties he had received from it. Antony eventually discovered that his pay had been sent to <u>Anthony</u> Holland (who was by that time deceased), and ended up being given to charity. Antony felt that his needs were greater than the charity, The Screen Actors' Guild, and he got the money refunded.

As 1985 approached, Antony's tenure at Studio 58 was drawing to a close. There had been many good years but, almost inevitably, there had been some disasters. One very difficult group of first-year students had staged a rebellion and demanded changes. They had intimated that they were dissatisfied with the quality of the program and had wanted the right to choose their own plays and set their own schedule. A committee was struck to hear their grievances but this made discipline very difficult and took a lot of time and energy away from the program. In the end the committee dismissed all the complaints as entirely without merit and completely exonerated Antony and his team. However, Antony was solely responsible for end of year grading and for deciding which of the students would qualify to continue into the second year. On this occasion only two students passed. Antony is unapologetic, insisting that the reason the other students complained, and ultimately failed, was that they lacked the talent and commitment necessary to become actors.

Denise Golemblaski was an administrative assistant at Langara during Antony's final days at Studio 58 and she vividly recalls his 65th. birthday when he was front and centre: toasted and roasted. While he was standing in the middle of the faculty lounge holding a large bouquet of balloons Denise had, in one brief moment, a vision of Antony as he must have been as a child; quiet, shy, innocent and trusting that everything would be all right on the night.

But everything was not all right. It was the spring of 1985 and, after twenty years service to VCC and Langara, Antony had reached mandatory retirement age and was being told that he had to take a final bow.

Retirement at any age was not something Antony had in mind and he wasn't going without a fight. He consulted a lawyer and he went kicking and screaming to the press. Max Wyman, the Arts Columnist of The Province newspaper, did a lengthy piece headed "Stupid" in which Antony decried the fact that he was being forced to retire; insisting that he still had a great deal to offer – a statement borne out by the fact that he was still teaching a quarter of a century later, though not at Langara.

However, neither the law nor public pressure swayed the administration at Langara and Antony began preparing for his swansong: Keith Dewhurst's play *Lark Rise to Candleford* directed by his wife, Catherine Cains. The play is set in a late Victorian English village where the actors mingle with the audience in a large space without staging or seats. Antony said of the play at the time, "It's a great challenge to the actors because it breaks all the rules and guidelines and allows something quite magical to happen".

'Breaking the rules' is something that Antony had always been good at, but the 'Retirement at 65' rule was one that he couldn't get around, and the final curtain came down on his twenty-year run as the Founder and Director of Studio 58 in the summer of 1985.

Act 17

(Un)Happy Retirement

And so he plays his part. The sixth age shifts
Into the lean and slipper'd pantaloon,
With spectacles on nose and pouch on side,
His youthful hose, well saved, a world too wide
For his shrunk shank; and his big manly voice,
Turning again toward childish treble, pipes
And whistles in his sound.

(Shak. As You Like It)

Antony Holland wasn't ready to shift into the lean and slipper'd pantaloon. He hadn't planned to retire – ever. Like Bette Davis, he had done it the hard way and he had no thought of letting go of his achievements at Langara. He had almost single-handedly created one of the most respected theatre schools in North America and now he was being shown the door, and he faced an uncertain future.

Catherine, his second wife, didn't want to stay in Vancouver. She had friends in Deep Cove, northeast of the city, where she had lived with her first husband, and wanted to return there, and so began an unsettling period of time for Antony when he would desperately try to fit into a new role and attempt to resurrect his previously winning formula. All he needed was a new venue, a new cast, and a re-hashed script, and he could once again put on a show that would astonish the masses.

A modeling studio run by Ramona Beauchamp was his first venue and, together with Catherine, he set up The Ramona Beauchamp

155

Theatre School. Antony had confused the proprietor of the studio with a social activist and, too late, discovered that she was a grasping woman with financial problems who had little interest in helping up and coming actors and had made the course far too expensive for the majority of potential students.

After a disappointing and unsuccessful year with Ramona Beauchamp, Antony and Catherine started their own school at the home of the North Vancouver Community Arts Council. Their 'Film and Theatre School of Presentation House' offered full-time courses, by audition, and attracted many students who had been with them at Studio 58 and the University of British Columbia.

Plays such as *A Midsummer Night's Dream* and *Romeo and Juliet* at Presentation House form the earliest memories of Antony's granddaughter, Jasmine. She was just six years old when Antony introduced her to the theatre (and to the delights of fine dining in fancy restaurants), and she thoroughly enjoyed the experience. When Jasmine was nine she auditioned for a part in a production of *Macbeth* and she played the role of MacDuff's son. She says, "This was truly a magical time in my childhood and I loved every moment of the experience and was grateful for the opportunity."

However, the 'Film and Theatre School of Presentation House' turned out to be a less magical experience for Antony and Catherine. In business they were exactly the opposite of Ms. Beauchamp and put more emphasis on the acting acumen of students than their ability to pay. Consequently the school became a financial burden. In the end the enterprise was supported by Catherine, who continued working at UBC, and by Antony's appearances on the professional stage and in movies.

Antony's most memorable movie moment came in 1985 when he acted alongside four-time Oscar winner Katharine Hepburn (The American Film Institute's greatest female star of all time) in the made-for-TV movie, *Mrs. Dellafield Wants to Marry*, directed by George Schaefer.

Schaefer held a script reading and Katharine Hepburn arrived already 'off-book' so, while everyone else sat to read, the seventy nine year old screen goddess astounded them all by standing to act her part.

In the movie, Hepburn plays an aging widow who wants to marry a Jew, but her adult children object – fearing they will lose their inheritance. Her deceased husband is named Spud and in the script Mrs. Dellafield tells her children, "I loved Spud with all my heart". However, at the reading Hepburn incorrectly said, "I loved Spence with all my heart".

It was a Freudian slip that caused a ripple around the room. Everyone knew of Hepburn's lengthy love affair with Spencer Tracy, and one cast member was so moved that she began crying and couldn't stop. Katharine Hepburn didn't realize she had made the faux pas and carried on.

Antony had a short scene as a disapproving protestant clergyman, and the shooting was to take place in the upstairs room of a large manor house. On the first call Antony sat in the dressing room all day before being told that the shooting was finished for the day because Ms. Hepburn wanted different furniture. He was recalled a few days later and, following make-up and wardrobe, he watched while a very bad actor repeatedly messed up his lines until Katharine Hepburn finally called it a day because she was tired.

Antony now had two days' pay for doing nothing, but, third time lucky, and everything was going well until he had a panic attack. Just as the cameras were about to roll he was overwhelmed by the thought of appearing with the greatest movie actress of all time and he froze ...

Vancouver
1986

Dear Friend

I thought Bette Davis was the Queen, but Katharine Hepburn was an absolute Goddess. As Romeo says, "*See, how she leans her cheek upon her hand! O, that I were a glove upon that hand, That I might touch that cheek!*"

I was so enthralled that my knees turned to jelly and my tongue got knotted. She must've realized because she asked me if I minded running lines a couple of times.

Did I mind? Did I mind? What a relief, but I was still stiff as a board so she suggested that we walk into the room together rather than just sitting at the desk. Schaefer agreed, and while the lights were reset she asked me what I thought of the script. "I might have changed one line…" I started, and in no time at all she made Schaefer take out his pen.

Our first take was so-so, but she thought that my character would be showing his feelings a bit more. That did it – it was a wrap.

I still can't believe it. In just one hour the greatest movie actress of all time calmed me down, built me up, expanded my part, got the director to change my lines and gave me a valuable acting lesson. Now that's the kind of instructor I need at my school … I wonder what she would charge?

Antony

Antony was so star-struck by Hepburn that he couldn't resist telling her of two occasions they had been to the theatre together. In 1953, when Richard Burton was playing *Hamlet* at The Old Vic, Antony had watched her walk down the theatre's aisle on the arm of Robert Helpmann, the principal dancer of the Sadler's Wells Ballet, and years later, again in London, they both saw Alec McCowen performing a solo recitation of *The Gospel According to St Mark* (an amazing feat of memory which was outmatched by Antony in 2010 when he learned and recited the *Gospel* in its entirety at the age of ninety!). Needless to say, Katharine Hepburn had no recollection of Antony at either event.

Antony's second wife, Catherine, was a socialite, and was considerably younger than Antony, so she wanted to party. But Antony was now nearing seventy and, while he still enjoyed ballroom dancing, he was well past partying in nightclubs and gay bars. Catherine, on the other hand, spent more and more time in the company of a gay male friend who would deliver her home late at night, intoxicated. Antony admits that he was troubled by his wife's alleged plutonic relationship with another man, and their marriage was starting to fall apart.

And then, while making the 1989 movie, *Cousins,* directed by Joel Schumacher, Antony fell head over heels for another woman. He was playing a priest at a wedding and he fell in love with one of the guests: Isabella Rossellini, (daughter of Swedish actress Ingrid Bergman and famed Italian director, Roberto Rossellini). Sadly, for Antony, Isabella never knew about his crush and never even spoke to him.

The situation on the home front should have improved when Catherine's gay friend moved to New Zealand, but the waters were muddied when Catherine persuaded Antony to buy the man's house. The property overlooked Indian Arm, a lake-like fjord surrounded by steep, forested cliffs. It was picturesque, but this was a bad time for Antony: 'The Film and Theatre School of Presentation House' was failing; he missed his work at Studio 58; missed the social connections to the students and faculty; and, in particular, missed the financial stability it had provided. Catherine was spending more and more while earning less and less and Antony became depressed.

Perhaps Antony's greatest strength is his self-discipline. As his daughter says, "No compromising – He stuck to his path whatever." But by the end of the eighties he had lost direction and his life was floundering out of control. And then a storm brought down the hillside close to the house. The house was undamaged but Catherine was terrified that it would happen again and she wanted to move to Gabriola Island where Antony owned some land and a small vacation cabin.

Catherine's plan was to buy a farm on the island and grow vegetables, but Antony's dream of being a market gardener had died many years before on his arrival in Canada and he wasn't keen to try again. However, under pressure, he agreed to visit Gabriola and view a number of potential farms. They visited and Antony spotted what appeared to be an ideal property – a house with a little land, though certainly not a farm. It wasn't at all what Catherine had in mind, but Antony was struggling to get his life back under his own control and he bought it.

While Gabriola Island is a dream vacation and retirement location just off the coast of Vancouver, it is not an easy place to get to or from in a hurry. Antony was faced with that problem soon after moving to the island in 1990.

Bingo, an American movie starring a dog, was being filmed in Vancouver and Antony had auditioned for the part of a veterinary surgeon. His shoot was planned for a particular Saturday but the assistant director phoned on the preceding Wednesday and said he was needed immediately. Vancouver is a two-ferry trip from Gabriola Island that takes a minimum of four hours, so the studio sent a helicopter. It was the star treatment, and the experience of flying serenely across the Strait of Georgia just above the waves and landing on a beach to be met by a limousine with flashing lights was so magical that the following year he took Catherine on a sightseeing flight in Hawaii. She was petrified, but Antony assured her that it would be as relaxing as a gentle massage. He was wrong – the helicopter pilot was a daredevil who skimmed the tops of mountains, dropped into steep ravines and flung the machine around the sky in a stomach-churning aerial ballet.

The flight turned out to be as disastrous as the movie, best described by one reviewer as "stunningly unwatchable", and Antony was disappointed that, despite his best efforts to buy up all the copies, some escaped.

On a later occasion, the inaccessibility of Gabriola Island almost cost Antony a role in *Yes Virginia, There is a Santa Claus,* starring Richard Thomas, Edward Asner and Charles Bronson. Vancouver was a long way to go to audition for a very small part that he neither wanted nor was suited for, but his agent was persuasive. As Antony was leaving the audition room, confident that he had failed to impress the director and his two assistants, a voice from behind him said, "Didn't you play Shylock in England some years ago?" Antony had last performed *The Merchant* in the U.K. in 1947, more than forty four years earlier, and he spun around in surprise. The director was Charles Jarrott (winner of the Golden Globe for *Anne of a Thousand Days* in 1969), and not only had he seen Antony's portrayal of Shylock with The West of England Theatre Company in 1947, but he had been the ASM on the production. It had been his first job in theatre. The connection paid off. Not only did Antony get the part, but Jarrot expanded the role for him.

Antony wasn't always so fortunate. For instance: in *Legends of the Fall* with Brad Pitt and Antony Hopkins, he had the part of a schooner captain off the coast of Jamaica. All went well in rehearsal, with a calm sea, light winds and a professional skipper by his side, but when the cameras rolled the wind picked up and left Antony clinging to the wheel. Antony proudly told all his friends and acquaintances about his role with Brad Pitt before he discovered that his scene had ended up on the cutting room floor.

Jasmine, Antony's eldest granddaughter, also suffered when he and Catherine moved to Gabriola Island. Despite Antony wanting to have a closer connection with Jasmine than he had with her father (his son, Nelson) the island's relative inaccessibility made this difficult. However, in spite of negative impressions Jasmine was given by other family members, she was determined to be open towards Antony. She says, "I was raised to embrace my grandfather with caution yet, after my wedding at the age of twenty two, my husband and I spent a few days at my grandfather's home and I marveled at his stories and, as an adult, felt free to enjoy what he had to offer. I also learned quickly that he was an excellent cook, and was as protective of his domain in the kitchen as my grandmother, and that he loved to garden just as she did."

Unfortunately, now that Antony had moved to Gabriola Island he quickly became, in Catherine's eyes, grey, old and miserable. He was depressed. The bills were continually piling up as he desperately tried to placate his much younger wife. He extended the house, added a library and built additional rooms for her, and he built her an enormous stone fireplace just like one she had seen in an English pub. But the money was bleeding faster than he could replenish it. He upped the mortgage, but

Catherine constantly maxed out the credit cards.

Antony would often spend all day travelling to and from Vancouver for a five minute audition that frequently resulted in roles that paid less than the expenses incurred, and although Catherine got a job in theatre-arts at Malaspina University College on Vancouver Island, she soon fell out with the artistic director. Today Antony wryly comments, "Catherine had a habit of falling out with people."

By the mid nineteen nineties, with a degree of desperation, the couple started another theatre school, this time offering evening classes in a dance studio in Nanaimo on Vancouver Island. One of Catherine's friends had wanted to be a partner, supposedly to teach puppetry, and had offered to get another friend to make a business plan for the school. Antony saw no point in having a business plan – he had been running theatre schools since 1949 – but Catherine insisted. However, things quickly went sour when Antony discovered that he had been deceived by Catherine and her friend. The proposed partner had no skill or interest in puppetry but had wanted to teach acting. However, both women had correctly guessed that Antony would not want her as an acting instructor so had planned the puppetry as a ruse.

As soon as Antony discovered the subterfuge he pulled out of the partnership and got saddled with a bill for $12,000 for the business plan that he had neither needed nor wanted, thereby exacerbating his financial problems.

The theatre school in Nanaimo was yet another financial failure and Catherine took some part-time work in a private film school in Vancouver to bring in an income. She rented a houseboat for accommodation, but by the time she had paid all her expenses there was no money left and she was eventually forced to return to Gabriola and surrender her credit cards. But Antony would not, and could not, give up. There were debts to be paid. In any case, it simply wasn't in his nature to accept defeat and, although he was in his mid seventies, he decided to go back to the drawing board and start over. He had a two story workshop in the grounds of his house on Gabriola Island which, he decided, could be converted into a small theatre school.

Tyler Page was one of the few students attracted to the island school and he rented a nearby house and kept warm by burning the previous occupant's abandoned furniture. Antony had little sympathy and told him that he didn't know cold till he had been to a nudist colony in England. However, after a few weeks the house was sold from under Tyler and he moved into Antony's studio loft in exchange for odd jobs. "I chopped wood, painted the studio, mowed the lawn, and even painted the inside of his house," says Tyler, "and yet, after all those hours of labour, I still owe Antony my life."

Like many aspiring actors, Tyler had little or no money and Antony spent sleepless nights trying to find ways to keep him and other students on the course without paying.

A bread bakery, albeit unregulated and unofficial, appears at first glance to be an unlikely money spinner, but Antony soon discovered that many Gabriolans were willing to buy his freshly made loaves to support his school.

Tyler Page benefited greatly from Antony's largesse and is today a successful props master in Vancouver. His most vivid memory of his time at The Gabriola Theatre School is Antony's mastery of fencing. Tyler had already practiced stage fighting so was surprised when Antony, already in his late seventies, shuffled into the room wearing a pair of old slippers and put on a mask. I can't hit an old man. He's old enough to be my great, great, grandfather, thought Tyler, at that time in his early twenties. But then, he says, "Antony saluted, dropped his mask, and went for me. When he had completely thrashed me, he took off his mask, saluted and shuffled off. Sometimes he just ignores you, but when he does engage Wow!"

Act 18

New Millennium - New Beginning!

Farewell! a long farewell, to all my greatness!
This is the state of man: today he puts forth
The tender leaves of hope; to-morrow blossoms,
And bears his blushing honours thick upon him;
The third day comes a frost, a killing frost,
And, when he thinks, good easy man, full surely
His greatness is a-ripening, nips his root,
And then he falls as I do. I have ventured,
Like little wanton boys that swim on bladders,
This many summers in a sea of glory,
But far beyond my depth: my high-blown pride
At length broke under me and now has left me,
Weary and old with service, to the mercy
Of a rude stream.

(Shak. Henry VIII)

In 1996 the Artistic Director at Chemainus Theatre on Vancouver Island hired Antony to direct George Bernard Shaw's *Arms and the Man,* and Antony, a confirmed atheist, was disturbed to discover that the theatre was being run by religious zealots who insisted on prayers before every rehearsal. However, he needed the money, so he gritted his teeth, said "Amen", and set to work. As rehearsals progressed Antony became increasingly concerned about one actress who seemed incapable of learning her lines, so he gave the role to his wife, Catherine.

This seemingly innocuous action was to have a profound effect on Antony's future because it would enable Catherine to meet, and later form a close relationship, with another woman – a woman who would eventually come between Antony and Catherine and would bring an end to their already rocky marriage.

The wheels of this complicated and subsequently injurious relationship moved slowly, and to the outside world Antony and Catherine may have appeared much as normal: they ran the acting school at The Gabriola Theatre Centre; they performed and directed together; they even socialized together – to a degree. But Catherine and her friend spent more and more time in each other's company, often under Antony's roof, and festering beneath the surface were the germs of a lengthy and bitter divorce.

Antony had long suspected that Catherine was having an affair with her gay male friend (although he had now married another man – with Catherine acting as *Best Man* (or *Best Woman*)), and he was now faced with the disquieting possibility that she actually preferred another woman. He was traumatized and became deeply depressed and, when he finally confronted Catherine and her girlfriend, they admitted being in a lesbian relationship …

Gabriola Island
1998

Dear Friend

    I am lost for words to express my wretchedness, and yet the Bard seems privy to my deepest cares:

For my particular grief is of so flood-gate and o'erbearing nature that it engluts and swallows other sorrows.

Crabbed age and youth cannot live together: Youth is full of pleasance, age is full of care; Youth like summer morn, age like winter weather. Youth is nimble, age is lame.

For sweetest things turn sourest by their deeds; Lilies that fester smell far worse than weeds.

When daisies pied and violets blue and lady-smocks all silver-white, and cuckoo-buds of yellow hue, do paint the meadows with delight, The cuckoo then, on every tree, mocks married men; for thus sings he, Cuckoo, Cuckoo; O word of fear, unpleasing to a married ear!

Such an act.... makes marriage-vows as false as dicers' oaths:

O tiger's heart wrapt in a woman's hide!

Take, O, take those lips away, that so sweetly were forsworn; And those eyes, the break of day, lights that do mislead the morn:

O, call back yesterday, bid time return.

Like a dull actor now, I have forgot my part, and I am out, even to a full disgrace.

Antony

By the turn of the century the situation was still unresolved. Catherine and her lesbian partner, along with various dogs, cats and children, were coming and going from Antony's house and his life. He was still desperately clinging onto his marriage, while Catherine was clearly clinging to Antony for the money. She was in no hurry to leave, not until she had extracted every last cent, and even then she would continue to draw deeply from the well.

The year was 2000... Antony Holland was eighty years old and it was time to put on a happy face. As Catherine says, "Antony keeps his feelings well hidden, except onstage when he is the master of emotions."

Birthdays have always been important to Antony and, to this day, he delights in having a party where he can perform sketches, ditties and songs to his friends, just as he did when he was eight years old at his home in Tiverton. His songs have changed over the years, and so have his sketches and tales. He now has a penchant for the risqué and a fondness for saying "fuck", and it doesn't take an observer long to realize that inside this elderly and wilting frame is still a young and mischievous little boy desperately seeking the attention of his peers. This should not be misconstrued – it is the very nature of the beast that Antony is, was, and always will be, an exhibitionist. Even when he is ensconced behind a newspaper at an audition or rehearsal, or falling asleep onstage, he somehow retains the ability to remain the focus of attention.

It has been suggested by some that Antony's craving for love and admiration may stem from his perceived lack of affection from his father in childhood. Only a psychologist could provide a definitive answer, but if this is the case then it is probable that the world at large has been the great beneficiary of the inner torment of an unloved child.

Tyler Page, a student at the Gabriola school during the difficult years in the late nineties, describes Antony as being aloof and distant. However, he adds, that beneath the frosty façade was a man worth meeting, saying, "My time spent with Antony was the most valuable thing I've ever done."

On August 22, 1999, Antony took his oft-played screen role as a priest seriously and carried out the wedding ceremony for Tyler and his wife, Jasmine. Tyler explains that they wanted to be married by someone wise, understanding, sentimental and realistic. "We wanted," he adds, "to be well wished into the future by a person we could emulate – a man so honest that he deliberately pronounced every single spelling mistake I had made in the wedding vows!"

Shawne Davidson, an ex-student of theatre-arts at Studio 58, visited Antony on Gabriola Island during the thorny years at the end of the nineties. Antony was in his late seventies at that time, was suffering with knee ailments in addition to marital discord, and Shawne was dismayed to see that he had lost some of the spring in his step. However, she was excited to discover that he lived near a riding stable and decided to book an afternoon's ride. "Make it two", said Antony when she called for a reservation, and Shawne was amazed. "I didn't know you rode!" she exclaimed. "I never have", he replied, with the twinkle of a young boy in his eye, "But you make it sound so exciting".

Unfortunately (or possibly fortunately for Antony), the stable was closed and they never got their ride, but Shawne says, "He taught me a huge lesson that day: always be open to new things, and never think you are too old to try something for the first time."

Antony had never thought that he was too old for anything, but as the new millennium dawned he was facing an uncertain future and the dark prospect of spending his golden years alone.

By the fall of 2000 Catherine had largely moved out of the marital home and was sharing a cabin with her lesbian partner. However, despite Antony's acceptance that his marriage was effectively over, the disagreement over the division of assets would keep the couple locked in a tortuous dance for some time to come …

Gabriola Island
September 2000

Dear Catherine

I cannot stop the tears. It is bad enough that you are unfaithful with another woman and want to take my house from under me, but now when you look at me I feel you mocking me as the Lord Chief-Justice mocked Falstaff:

Do you set down your name in the scroll of youth, that are written down old with all the characters of age? Have you not a moist eye? a dry hand? a yellow cheek? a white beard? a decreasing leg? an increasing belly? Is not your voice broken? your wind short? your chin double? your wit single? and every part about you blasted with antiquity? and will you yet call yourself young? Fie, fie, fie.

I am a man more sinned against than sinned, but I fear that the lawyers will side with you and leave me penniless. I agree with Dick in Henry VI, *The first thing we do, let's kill all the lawyers.*

You demand to keep everything I have given you; that I should pay all your debts, and you still want half of everything I own! *Blow, blow, thou winter wind. Thou art not so unkind as man's ingratitude.*

O God! that one might read the book of fate, And see the revolution of the times......O, if this were seen, The happiest youth, viewing his progress through, what perils past, what crosses to ensue, would shut the book, and sit him down and die.

I fear that I will suffer *the slings and arrows of outrageous fortune*, but I must extricate myself from this charade that we call marriage. As Shakespeare writes in the sonnets, *Farewell! (Catherine), thou art too dear for my possessing,*

Antony

The early part of the new millennium was especially hard on Antony. He was somewhat isolated and, although he was perfectly capable of living independently, he missed the companionship of a woman – especially an attractive one.

Antony has always had an appreciative eye for a beautiful woman and once, when auditioning potential students, a glamorous creature slithered onto the stage in front of him and caused him to drop his newspaper. The girl had the face for *Vogue* and the figure for *Playboy* and she ticked all of his boxes. And then she forgot her lines, couldn't talk, couldn't dance and couldn't act. But Antony wasn't giving up easily. "Can you sing?" he asked hopefully. "What?" she said. "Anything", he replied. "I don't know nothing", she answered, and he slowly and reluctantly crossed out the ticks and called, "Next!"

Layla Alizada is a beautiful woman who has no difficulty with her lines or acting, and in 2002 she played Cordelia to Antony's King Lear in her final year at Studio 58. She first met Antony as he painfully struggled up the stairs to the photo shoot for *Lear* and he seemed so fragile and soft-spoken that she doubted his ability to play the King. But, she says, "As soon as he was at home onstage he had enough energy to play Lear and all the other parts combined."

Antony, true to his Stanislavski principles, befriended Layla – she was, after all, his favourite daughter in the play – and, despite a sixty year age difference, theirs was an immediate bond. "He is one of the brightest, most youthful and vital people I have ever met," reports Layla who has remained friends with Antony to the present day.

Jane Heyman, a graduate of UBC and instructor at Langara College under Antony from 1977 – 1979, was the director of this particular three-week run of *King Lear* at Studio 58, and was concerned during the auditioning process as Antony appeared to be particularly frail.

Allan Morgan was chosen to play Gloucester but, because of Antony's age and apparent frailty, Jane quietly asked Alan to learn both parts so that he could take over the lead role if necessary. However, Antony turned up at first rehearsal, already off book, and he walked onstage and lit up. His acting, as always, was simple and moving, but he was demanding and specific. He brought a lifetime's experience to the production and he had a profound effect on the students. One student was twice late onstage and Jane ordered him to stay backstage during every rehearsal and watch carefully. By watching Antony perform, the student caught on, changed his attitude and mended his ways. As Jane says, "He'd learnt an important lesson from a very old man."

Jane found it a great pleasure to work with Antony and says that her favourite part is when Lear runs onstage barefoot in a nightgown with flowers in his hair. Antony, at eighty two and suffering from knee problems, came running onstage on tiptoes.

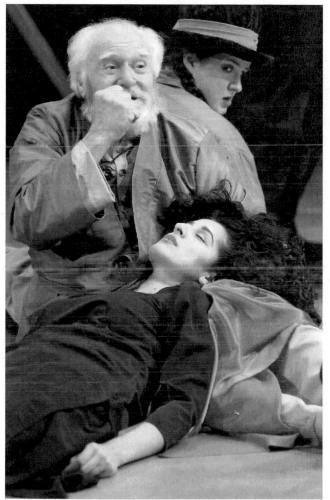

Photo – David Cooper. By kind permission of Studio 58, Langara College

Antony as Lear with Layla Alizada as Cornelia and Debbie Love as the Fool - King Lear 2002

Layla Alizada, Cordelia in *Lear*, kept in touch with Antony after the run and Antony would often stay with her and her partner, Ocean Mussack, when he was working on movies in Vancouver.

Antony was going through his divorce with Catherine at the time and, despite the enormous age difference between himself and the two young women, the three enjoyed a close friendship. They would go for dinners, watch old movies and talk a lot, completely incognizant of the generation gulf. But these were emotional days for Antony as he contemplated a lonely future, and on one occasion as he sought Ocean's advice on his marital problems he began to cry.

Antony is a profoundly emotional man who usually presents a composed, almost laissez-faire, face to the world irrespective of his inner turmoil. But when his wounds are exposed he is prone to uncontrollable weeping, sometimes lasting hours. Ocean was initially at a loss when confronted by Antony's sobbing, but she eventually offered a slice of chocolate ganache cake and a box of tissues – just as she would do with any of her girlfriends in a similar situation. Antony laughed, wiped his eyes and ate the cake.

Antony may have been able to compose himself on this occasion, but as the state of his marriage continued to deteriorate he would spend many hours grieving alone. But life for Catherine wasn't always easy either. She eventually fell out with her lesbian partner and moved back in with Antony in 2002. However, too much damage had been done for the relationship to survive and the couple finally separated in June of 2003 and divorced the following December.

One of the movies that Antony made in Vancouver during the time of this emotional upheaval was *The National Lampoon's Thanksgiving Family Reunion,* a made-for-TV movie directed by Neal Israel, and Antony was chosen for the role of Uncle Phil.

Antony had been promised several weeks work on the movie, but his heart sank on the first day when he discovered that his car had been stolen and he couldn't get to the set. Despite the renowned parsimoniousness of the producer, the studio sent a car to collect him – an honour usually reserved for important American stars …

Vancouver
2003

Dear Friend

I can't believe it. A decent run of work to pay off some bills and someone stole my car.

I was hoping that, finally, I would get a movie part that I could really get my teeth into, but I'm playing a toothless old codger and most of the time all I have to do is fart – actually I just pull faces and the special effects boys add the raspberries later. This is not Shakespeare!

Anyway, during the shoot I was awarded a lifetime service award by the Union of BC Performers, so I wrote to the director and said I thought I should get some recognition like:

a) Double salary,

b) An unrestricted set pass

or, c) A very attractive and obliging young assistant – just like the stars are afforded.

He circled (c) and sent a very nice young man who offered to clean my car. "If you can find it – you can clean it," I said, but he didn't.

As Claudius says in Hamlet, *"When sorrows come, they come not single spies but in battalions,"* and halfway through the shoot I was called to the office and they said I couldn't continue filming until I passed a medical exam for insurance purposes. "Medical insurance?" I queried, "Why do I need medical insurance? It's not dangerous. I'm only farting!" But they insisted and, guess what, I failed. The Doc said I had a heart murmur. Luckily, there was nothing wrong with my ass so they let me carry on farting without insurance.

Antony

Antony's supposed heart murmur was concerning, but he later saw his own doctor who assured him that he'd probably had it all his life and that it was nothing to worry about.

Antony's eyesight is something else that he generally doesn't have to worry about, (although in 2010 he began seeing visions and was diagnosed with age-related macular degeneration). However, in the 2004 American TV series *Kingdom Hospital,* written by the science-fiction/horror legend, Stephen King, Antony played an elderly hospital patient, but, despite his advanced age, the director thought his eyes looked too young for the part and wanted him to wear clouded contact lenses. Sensing Antony's concern the director said, "Don't worry. I'll send a very nice young assistant to put them in and take them out for you". Antony's hopes were again dashed when another young man showed up.

Diane Ladd, a thrice-nominated Oscar contender, played the woman psychic throughout the series of *Kingdom Hospital* but, off-screen, she actually was a psychic and so she made up the dialogue as she went along. Antony never knew what she would say next, and never knew how best to respond, so one shoot went from 10am one day until 4am the following morning and Antony, by his own admission, eventually drifted asleep and had to be woken.

Whenever Antony had movie shoots or plays in Vancouver he would usually stay with ex-students, and so it was in 2002 that he stayed with Denise Golemblaski who was rabbit-sitting for a friend at the time. Knowing Antony's commitment to his work, Denise wasn't at all surprised to find him running his lines before dawn one morning, but she was intrigued to find that the rabbit, imaginatively named 'Bunny', was sitting quietly by his side on the settee taking in every word.

Antony's commitment and dedication to his craft is legendary and Lynna Goldhar recalls his one-man show, titled *Sharing Shakespeare,* when she and Antony arrived at the Vancouver theatre for a matinee and discovered that only three people had bought tickets. The show had been well attended up to that time so it was very disappointing. Small houses are notoriously difficult and draining and Lynna wanted to cancel because eighty three year old Antony had another performance later that evening. Antony wouldn't hear of it, reminding Lynna that three people had paid to be entertained, and entertained they would be. In Lynna's own words: "Antony delivered the entire play to this elderly trio as if they were friends. It was so natural and intimate that it was easy to forget we were at the theatre. One of the women actually asked him some direct questions during the performance and, without skipping a beat, he simply answered. She thanked him and he carried on."

This concern for the audience is something that Antony learned, in a way, from Sir Laurence Olivier. Whenever Olivier got stage fright (which he often did, especially toward the end of his career when he was convinced that he would never be perfect), his mantra would be, 'I'll teach those hostile bastards'. Antony, on the other hand, would spin this around and think: These people are my friends. They want things to be good, so I must make sure they are. My guardian angel is with me – both in life and on the stage. I have taken huge risks and my guardian angel has always taken care of me. "It's nonsense really," admits Antony, "But it works for me. And it takes away the fear."

Considering Antony's age and experience it is difficult to believe that being in the public eye would ever frighten him. By necessity he is a shameless self-promoter who courts publicity whenever he has the opportunity. Bruce Mason was the reporter for the Gabriola Sounder newspaper from 2002 – 2009 and filed many stories about Antony during that time. Today, he writes of Antony – A Star Turn on Gabriola Island:

"His reputation was considerable, even legendary. And although it preceded him, nothing could have prepared me for my first up-close encounter with Antony Holland.

"Care to purchase a pavlova?" he enquired, one hand outstretched, the other pointing somewhat dramatically to a basket containing a selection of baked goods suspended on his arm. As always, a minimum of props was all that he required to make a lasting impression, in this case, a few loaves to cue an entrance of ongoing acts featuring wit, wisdom and assorted killer quotes that helped sustain me and the stories I was writing for the community newspaper.

Holland was selling his wares fresh from the baker's oven that he had installed backstage to help finance the theatre revolution he was staging and waging, starting front and centre in his charming clapboard facility in a forest on Gabriola Island.

"Not only does he advise me on what to read, but what to eat as well," reported the owner of the art gallery where I had arranged to interview Holland, and she selected a minimalist whole-wheat concoction from the basket while I searched for coins to pay for my pastry.

"Among other things, theatre provides an opportunity to hold out a mirror on the world for those who choose to look and in some cases lives have been changed mightily by the experience," Holland said, sipping a latte as I struggled with a parched ballpoint pen, but there would never be enough ink.

"Not another piece on Antony Holland?" the editor of the Gabriola Sounder frequently pleaded with me, nervously scanning the weekly lists of stories I was proposing to file in a mad seven year dash to earn enough to claw my way above the poverty line.

My first story with him was culled from a telephone conversation in April, 2002, when his newly purchased, previously-owned and recently repaired, VW van caught fire on Buttercup Road. "It must be some kind of record. We bought it on Monday, insured it on Tuesday, and lost it on Wednesday," he informed me. "Had some papers in the back; damned inconvenient," he added.

It seemed there would always be papers when we met – some present; some missing – scripts from the thousands he had filed away; an equal number of reviews and photographs from decades on the stage; numerous drafts of ads for endless upcoming productions that he thought were especially relevant right now; and names of cast members, cobbled together from lists of professional colleagues and former students residing in Vancouver, Victoria and further afield. Invariably there would be Gabriolans; a 3-D parade of characters appearing out of the woodwork and seizing an opportunity to realize long lost dreams of performing on the stage.

"The gist of the thing" he is fond of saying in reference to his No Bells and Whistles approach to art and life. No need to rehearse endlessly; fuss with lights and sound; marks and costumes. Enthusiasm is essential, however, on and off stage.

We watched in awe while his appetite for life grew rather than diminished as his age advanced far beyond three score and ten. "I am finding many more roles in my mid eighties," he had reported when I got my pen working during the first of many interviews. "There is far less competition and I can tell you that I am getting very good at coughing a lot and dying on stage." As time went by there would be other lines, tossed off spontaneously to entertain, enlighten and above all provide perspective to me and readers of our community newspaper. He reminded us to laugh and cry, many, many times.

When the island community decided to honour Holland in a ceremony on Gabriola, dubbing him: Sir Antony, Knight of the Realm and Bard of the Isles, he replied, "I can kneel, but I'm not certain I can get up afterwards", quoting Peter Ustinov. But there was a glitch: "Apparently we have to do it all again because they forgot to ask me if I accepted the honour", he joked, eagerly preparing for a repeat performance.

Once, when The Islands Trust announced its intention to restrict house concerts and performances, observers scratched their heads incredulously, wondering how love of music or Shakespeare could ever be legislated. A public information meeting was convened to discuss what appeared to be an insane proposal, especially in a place proudly proclaimed as the 'Isle of the Arts', and Holland stood before the elected officials and said, "Perhaps, given my age, you would consider great-grandfathering my theatre into your legislation. I'm not doing it for tourists, but for the residents, who seem to need some sort entertainment during the winter".

Permission was granted to allow Antony Holland to continue, because, after all, he had been staging plays on the island for years.

While others may debate whether Lear or Morrie was his greatest role, on the island his great achievements have been as a role-model and mentor. His zest for life has been an essential ingredient to this community and his passionate performance has transcended even his love of acting and live theatre. Like virtually everyone on Gabriola I sometimes suspect that Antony Holland will outlive us all. His legacy most certainly will."*

At the Haiti Benefit 2010 Gabriola Island

Photo – Courtesy of the Gabriola Sounder

*Bruce Mason – "Antony Holland. A Star Turn on Gabriola Island".

Act 19

Love in Autumn

Jack shall have Jill;
Nought shall go ill;
The man shall have his mare again,
And all shall be well.

(Shak. A Midsummer Night's Dream)

Photo – David Blue. Published with permission of Bard on the Beach

Antony as Adam and Tobias Slezak as Orlando in *As You Like It* – Bard on the Beach, Vancouver, 2005

Since 1990, Shakespeare lovers have been entertained by some of the finest productions of his work at Vancouver's celebrated 'Bard on the Beach.' The annual summer-long festival takes place under canvas in Vanier Park on Vancouver's beautiful waterfront and attendances exceed ninety thousand each season.

Bristol Old Vic Theatre School graduate Christopher Gaze is the Founder and Artistic Director of the 'Bard' and he says, "In 2005 we had a glorious summer with Antony playing Adam in *As You Like It*. He was eighty five years old and was totally reliable and always prepared. He was very dignified, and he was a mentor to younger actors – offering them helpful insights, and he was simply thrilled to be on the main stage."

Lara Gilchrist was playing Rosalind in that production of *As You Like It* and she says that this was the first time she really connected with Antony, despite the fact that they had both participated in Langara College's 2002 production of *King Lear* when she was still a student at Studio 58.

Lara recalls that one reviewer had difficulty hearing Antony on the opening night of *As You Like It* at the 'Bard' and suggested that he was too old for such a big theatre. Antony immediately sent a refutation to the newspaper explaining that he had swallowed a fly before going onstage and his muted performance had nothing to do with his age. The reviewer wrote an apology and Antony was enormously pleased with himself, but Lara wondered what he would have said to her had she done the same. "He always has a sharp tongue," she says, "Whether it's insulting how I say a line, or how I live my life, he's sure to tell me his opinion, so he would have given me flack for doing that."

To this day Antony insists that he really had swallowed a fly on this occasion (but he also insists that he has never fallen asleep onstage!).

When Antony was teaching he always advised his students to never take any notice of reviews, but one critique stung him badly. In the mid seventies with The Arts Club Theatre, Vancouver, he played a prison guard in *Fortune and Men's Eyes*, a 1967 play by John Herbert. Drawing on his experience at the Haney Correctional Institute, Antony knew exactly how guards behaved and portrayed a firm but fair-minded man who was concerned for the prisoners' welfare. However, the public perception of prison guards is always of tough bullies who wreak society's revenge on the inmates, and the drama critic of The Vancouver Sun, Lloyd Dyck, lambasted Antony for misunderstanding the character. This was a slight on Antony's acting ability, as well as his knowledge of prison life, that he never forgot.

Some twenty five years later *Fortune and Men's Eyes* was produced in New York, and a writer in Toronto's Globe and Mail said that the play had never been performed in Canada because its themes of homosexuality and sexual slavery were too disturbing. Antony was unaware of this article, but a few days later the newspaper printed a rebuttal from the President of the Theatre Critics of Alberta, saying, "I saw this play in the mid seventies in Vancouver, and no less a person than veteran Canadian actor, Antony Holland, brought the play to life as the prison guard". After more than a quarter of a century Antony was vindicated.

Following the 2005 season at 'Bard on the Beach,' Lara Gilchrist became a frequent visitor to the Gabriola Theatre Centre where she would be cajoled into play readings or helping in the garden. She says, "Antony always seems to get what he wants, but being in Antony's home as a guest is wonderful. He taught me how to plant and pull up potatoes, and there are freshly baked scones and bread everyday. And there is always a guilt trip for sleeping past 7:30am… and then there are the stories."

Antony is an inveterate, and accomplished, raconteur and Lara remembers tears flowing down his cheeks as he described taking the train through Provence after the war and seeing green for the first time in five years, and she says, "There are few of Antony's stories that I haven't heard twice but, after all the time I've spent with him, I'm not sure if he knows anything about me at all."

The restaurant/ballroom at Harrison Hot Springs, a spa resort east of Vancouver, has been Antony's haunt for decades and Lara is just one of the many dance partners he has taken there over the years. He is as much an exhibitionist on the dance floor as he is onstage – everyone knows his name and the band members all chat to him and play his favourites – but by 2010 his progressively worsening arthritis cramped his style and instead of twirling Lara around the floor he stood, dancing on the spot, motioning with his hand for her to spin, or walk this way or that. The crowd loved it and Antony played to them by announcing, "The man is always in control".

Lara, in her twenties, says Antony soaks up every moment of the experience and basks in the adoration of the onlookers, explaining:

"Every time someone says he is an inspiration, or how much they love watching us, Antony tells them right away what he does and who he is. I enjoy leading them on by not revealing whether I am his daughter, granddaughter or lover, but once when I wore a fairly short dress Antony told me very seriously that he thought people were wondering if he had paid for me. He is always a charmer!"

Layla Alizada, another ex-student from Studio 58, has also been a regular dance partner at Harrison Hot Springs although she now lives in Los Angeles. "Antony's a wonderful dancer and claims that I'm one of his favourite dance partners," she says, though adds, "But I'm sure he says that to all the girls." On their last visit to Harrison Antony was having knee trouble and Layla considered pushing him around in a wheelchair as a joke.

The 'old guy in a wheelchair' is not a part Antony relishes, or even considers, despite ongoing knee problems. However, it was a part he played successfully in 2008 when he arrived at Vancouver Airport to fly to Thunder Bay. He was in a wheelchair (to save his knees on the long walk to the gate) when he realized that he didn't have photo identification with him and wouldn't be allowed to fly. So he put on his acting cloak and did a very convincing performance of a senile old man – and they let him onto the plane.

Over the years Antony has produced and directed many plays by celebrated British playwright Sir Alan Ayckbourn and has established a relationship with him. He has acted in only one of Ayckbourn's plays because of a dearth of elderly characters, so he telephoned the playwright to complain.

"Ayckbourn suggested the old guy in a wheelchair in *Intimate Exchanges*," says Antony "But I reminded him that the guy has virtually no lines," and then he muses to himself, "Maybe it is time I thought of playing that part now."

However, in 2005 Antony had no such thought of playing an old man's part when he met Leslie Parrott. Leslie was taking a writing course at Malaspina University College (now Vancouver Island University) in Nanaimo when Antony saw her perform some of her comedy pieces and he was immediately impressed.

Leslie was sharing a house with another person at the time and was writing in the garage, while on e of Catherine's sons was renting Antony's house while he lived in the studio. So Antony reclaimed his house and hired Leslie as a housekeeper. Despite the age disparity (or perhaps, because of it) Antony became increasingly enamoured with Leslie and eventually invited her to stay with him ...

The Gabriola Theatre Centre
Gabriola Island
2005

Dear Friend

" *To be, or not to be: that is the question.*" Should I yet again risk my heart and my home? Leslie is a beautiful woman and I am very fond of her, but the warning words of Hamlet to Queen Gertrude make me pause: "*Ha! Have you eyes? You cannot call it love; for at your age the hey-day in the blood is tame, it's humble, And waits upon the judgment.*"

But then I am reminded of Adam in As You Like It. "*Be comfort to my age! Here is the gold; And all this I give you. Let me be your servant: Though I look old, yet I am strong and lusty... Therefore my age is as a lusty winter, Frosty, but kindly: let me go with you; I'll do the service of a younger man in all your business and necessities.*"

And I would make the argument that Duke Orsino makes in Twelfth Night:
"*Let still the woman take an elder than herself: so wears she to him, So sways she level in her husband's heart: For, boy, however we do praise ourselves, Our fancies are more giddy and unfirm, More longing, wavering, sooner lost and worn, Than women's are.*"

But, in truth, every time I think of asking Leslie to marry me I think of the words of King Lear: "*I am a very foolish fond old man. Fourscore and upward, not an hour more or less; And, to deal plainly, I fear I am not in my perfect mind.*"

Antony

In 2005 Leslie was a middle-aged writer struggling to keep a roof over her head, while Antony, at eighty five, was still working and trying to maintain a large property. It was a year before she accepted Antony's marriage proposal and she says that they came to each other's rescue and married on April 1, 2006 in relative secrecy. Here is how Leslie describes life in what she portrays as her 'front row seat' at *Antony – The Man*.

"My view is unsullied by firsthand knowledge of Antony's life prior to 2005, and what I see is quite remarkable. I said to him one evening, "You are the sanest person I have ever met," and of all the compliments he's ever received I think he was least prepared for that. Antony is a self-made man driven by a near indestructible engine which ticks over at a steady rate. He keeps the same pace with everything, from learning lines to setting 'live' mousetraps and emptying them at regular intervals throughout the night. The mice population may not have decreased, but somehow that doesn't matter. What matters is that he is doing something about it. The 'doing' part is what's important. When he set out to memorize *St. Mark's Gospel* at ninety he said that he had to believe he could do it. So the manuscript went with him everywhere: the ferry; the bus; his coffee klatch; the doctor's office; and even to his daughter's market where he sells his baked goods. He worked on it morning, noon and night, saying. "Learning lines is just work. There's nothing magical about it".

Antony is a doer. No Bells and Whistles* came into being because he picked up the phone and started the ball rolling. He wasn't concerned about the minutia or worried about failure, he just kept kicking that ball down the road. Procrastination is not in Antony's vocabulary, except when dealing with the books and papers piled on every available surface in the house. He is a pack rat – a sign of psychological maladjustment or simply his way of cherishing things that he treasures? Who knows... but he has filed away everything that was important to him since he was a teenager – not to enable him to live in the past, but so that he can be grounded and informed by it.

Antony cherishes his life; his experiences; the highs and lows... and the shows. Couple this with a curiosity that drives a voracious reading habit and you get a man with a wide-angle lens on most issues. I get frustrated and angry with what's going on in the world, while Antony

---

* No Bells and Whistles – the name of Antony's stripped-down performance company based at his Gabriola Theatre Centre.

remains pragmatic. He proudly polishes up his medals and attends the Remembrance Day services, yet he loathes war; he interacts amicably with political right-wingers, yet he abhors their views; he performs *St. Mark's Gospel* to appreciative groups of Evangelical Christians, yet he doesn't believe in God. It isn't simply that he's a good actor. He has an ability to slip through the different layers of society without making waves unless he sees an opportunity and causes things to happen.

Antony has brought many people into my life. He is more social than me and I realize, watching him, that you have to put energy into friends if they are important to you. He keeps in touch and offers help: a willing ear; an open-ended welcome. He shares special things: a good meal; clotted cream; homemade bread...and stories. Many of Antony's friends are in their twenties or thirties. They come to perform or just to visit and end up around the table, swapping stories. I used to think they'd rather be off to the bar but I was wrong. They love Antony's stories. He threads the past up into the present and gives them a sense of tradition in their profession; a feeling of pride and belonging. I don't think he 'holds court' out of sense of duty or mentorship; he needs these sessions as much as they do and that's what keeps them happening.

It hasn't been *entirely* easy to live with Antony. He knows what he wants and what makes him happy, and he surrounds himself in a vortex of energy which I was determined not to get sucked into. I was not going to become his 'Girl Friday' and refused to be his dancing partner. He accepted this, somewhat reluctantly, then picked up the phone and found other dancing partners.

Neither of us are good at dealing with confrontations so we descend into silence when we're hurt. Talking things out might be good for some people, but there is something to be said for taking responsibility for your own hurt feelings. We are alike in that respect and grow stronger because of it. Our home life is tranquil. We share a similar sense of humour – we laugh a lot and have great conversations. We have three dogs to fuss over and a huge garden which, under Antony's mentorship, has become more my domain than his. Thanks to Antony's love of cooking, we eat very well – although I once endured the grating voice of Julia Child for an entire week while he copied down recipes... but it was worth it!"

– – –

Antony introduced the 'No Bells and Whistles' concept to his Island Theatre Centre in 2006. His idea was to produce stripped-down performances without costumes or scenery in order to provide actors with performance opportunities, and audiences with an affordable theatre experience, without incurring the expense of staging full productions. In essence, the shows would be enhanced play readings with actors being responsible for 'creating' scenery and props in the minds of the audience. This concept particularly suited his performance space at the Gabriola Theatre Centre which has neither stage nor scenery flats.

The reviews were mixed; the actors' union objected to professionals working for nothing (even for readings), while some of the regular theatregoers didn't appreciate the oversimplified setting. However, as Lara Gilchrist discovered, Antony usually gets what he wants, and he persuaded the union to drop their complaint and, despite some grumblings, audiences were found. The high cost of ferrying actors to and from the island put a crimp in the ability to use many Vancouver actors in shows, but, at the end of the day, the No Bells and Whistles concept has been successful because of Antony's drive and enthusiasm.

Antony had initially moved to Gabriola Island in order to appease his second wife, but he became depressed because he felt isolated from the theatre community in Vancouver. However, he eventually came to understand that it wasn't so much his remoteness as it was his advancing years that caused him not to get parts. In his sixties and seventies he'd had no problem getting roles of priests and judges in movies, but society and times have changed; nowadays directors might take a thirty year old woman for those parts.

Antony says, "As you get older you get fewer and fewer parts until you get none at all," However, he did find some success as an aging accountant on the American television sitcom *The Chris Isaak Show* which ran from 2001 – 2004. The director had auditioned and found no one suitable until Isaak himself suggested Antony. The idea was originally ridiculed as Antony was in his early eighties at the time, but he was eventually offered the part and he put in a flawless performance.

And then came a role that was heaven sent for Antony; a role that would re-energize him and continue to bring him accolades and standing ovations into his nineties; a role that would come to define his later years, much as Danny in *Night Must Fall* had defined the very beginning of his professional career. In 2005 he was offered the part of Dr. Morris Swartz in Jeffrey Hatcher's adaptation of Mitch Albom's bestselling novel, *Tuesday's with Morrie*.

Photo – Courtesy of Jean Paul Photography

Antony preparing to 'die' as Morrie in Thunder Bay, Ontario (2008)

Act 20

'Tuesdays' with Antony

Last scene of all,
That ends this strange eventful history,
Is second childishness and mere oblivion,
Sans teeth, sans eyes, sans taste, sans everything.

(Shak. As You Like It)

The play *Tuesdays with Morrie* is an emotional account of the final chapter in the life of Professor Morris Swartz of Brandeis University, Boston, Massachusetts, who died from ALS* (Lou Gehrig's disease) in 1995. It is based on the experience of Mitch Albom, an ex-student, who visited Morrie every Tuesday in the last fourteen weeks of his life and learned many valuable life-lessons from his dying mentor.

By the spring of 2011 Antony Holland had 'died' as Morrie Swartz in front of some fifty thousand people during more than two hundred and fifty performances of *Tuesdays*. The play was an emotionally draining two-hander requiring particular stamina from Antony as he remained onstage throughout, yet, from Vancouver, British Columbia, to Tiverton, Devon, audiences had invariably given him a standing ovation and had always left the theatre in tears.

As for Antony: he too had shed a few tears over the play as it forced him to face the reality of his own mortality – something he had not done until he encountered Morrie in his late eighties.

*Amyotrophic lateral sclerosis.

Antony first performed *Tuesdays with Morrie* in Nanaimo, Vancouver Island, for The Western Edge Theatre Company, directed by Frank Moher, in 2005. The theatre was a dilapidated disused movie house with no dressing rooms or washrooms for the cast. The company had no money so the set was tatty, and the lights were a couple of fixed spotlights at the back of the auditorium. It was very reminiscent of some of the down-at-heel venues that Antony had performed in during his earliest days as an actor in Edwardian England. Antony had invited a number of ex-students to attend the opening night and Jan Hodgson, now stage manager with The Vancouver Playhouse, was horrified when she saw the conditions. However, she says that within the first five minutes of the performance she had completely forgotten about the surroundings.

The Nanaimo show was a great success and Bill Millerd, the Artistic Director of the Arts Club Theatre, Vancouver, showed interest in putting it onstage at his Granville Island theatre. Although Millerd was well aware of Antony's abilities the two hadn't worked together since 1985 at the time of Antony's enforced departure from Studio 58. The irony at that time was that the character Antony portrayed was a man who, like himself, was fighting against retirement. Now, more than twenty years later, Antony was portraying a much older man and Millerd had misgivings about employing a man in his late eighties to take on such a demanding role for a four-week run.

Millerd was finally convinced and Antony was quite happy with the $1,000 a week he was offered, until he later discovered that Warren Kimmel, the actor playing Mitch Albom, was getting considerably more. However, the play was very well received by both the public and the critics and, in June 2007, Antony was awarded the Jessie Richardson Award for 'Outstanding Performance by an Actor in a Lead Role – Large Theatre,' for his portrayal of the dying Morrie.

Tuesdays with Morrie was so successful that after four sold-out weeks at the Arts Club it was held over for another two weeks before going on a month-long tour of British Columbia.

Following the first run of *Tuesdays* at the Arts Club, the theatre opened an online notice board for patrons who wanted to publicly laud their own Morrie: the source of their inspiration; their hero. Many hundreds of people left touching tributes to friends and family members, and among them were several who named Antony, but one particularly poignant tribute stood out from all the others. It simply said, "ANTONY HOLLAND "My Greatest Teacher" *Catherine Mead"*.

Although Antony would always see himself as an actor, it is as a teacher that he would most like to be remembered. Many people owe their careers to Antony's tutoring, however he readily admits that his instructional style has been largely by intuition. "Every child is born with the talent to be an actor," he says, and he modestly claims that he has simply allowed students and performers to develop this talent with as little input or control as possible. His dictum could be *"By indirections find directions out"* as Lord Polonius commands Reynaldo in *Hamlet.*

By 2010, *Tuesdays with Morrie* starring Antony Holland had toured the length and breadth of British Columbia, from Victoria and Vancouver to Williams Lake, Penticton and Bowen Island, and had even delighted Ontarian audiences with a three-week run in Thunder Bay.

But then came disappointment...

The Tiverton Dramatic Society – the society that Antony had formed in his hometown in 1940 – was celebrating its 70th. anniversary in the summer of 2010 and so, seizing a perfect opportunity to both commemorate the society's longevity and to bookend his career, Antony offered to return to Tiverton to perform *Tuesdays with Morrie* under the organization's banner. While most associations might welcome their ninety year old founding father with open arms, the society decided that they were just too busy to accommodate him and said, "No thanks."

No one should be surprised to hear that Antony was undeterred by this refusal. Although deeply hurt, he did what he has done throughout his life whenever he has faced a barrier; he simply climbed over it. And so, at the age of ninety, and without the support of the society that he had brought to life as a twenty year old playing Danny in *Night Must Fall* in 1940, Albert Edwin (Antony) Holland returned to the land of his birth and performed *Tuesdays with Morrie* in Tiverton. The wheel had come full circle and, to cap off Antony's triumphant return, ninety two year old Dorothy Gunn (*née* Colebrook), the woman who exactly seventy years earlier had been persuaded by Antony to play Danny's ingénue, Olivia Grayne, was in the audience to watch another great performance and to wonder, along with Antony, where all those intervening years had gone.

Antony - Still dancing at 90 with his wife Leslie

Encore

Still Dancing at Ninety One

Tuesdays in Tiverton may have marked the end of Antony's career in England but, at the age of ninety one, he is still 'dying' onstage in the guise of Morrie Swartz in Canada, and he is still getting parts in movies and television shows – sometimes without trying.

In early 2011 his agent called to offer him an audition for a small role in a television series, but Antony wasn't particularly interested and after some thought decided not to attend. A few days later he received another call from his agent saying, "Congratulations. You got the part".

'I didn't go", Antony protested, but the series' director had seemingly worked with Antony in the past and had already decided that he was the only person for the role.

If *Tuesdays with Morrie* becomes Antony's stage swansong it is fitting that the character he plays is in many ways a reflection of himself. Morrie Swartz was a teacher, a philosopher and a pragmatist, who loved dancing, and it could be said that Antony, in true Stanislavski fashion, has studied for this role all of his life. However, there is one crucial divergence in that Antony does not have ALS.

One of Morrie's maxims that Antony can relate to is, "After you have wept and grieved for your physical losses, cherish the functions and the life you have left".

It is the spring of 2011 and Antony cherishes his life today. He is a playful nonagenarian with a sharp wit, a prodigious memory and a zest for life that would put many men half his age to shame. He currently has five touring shows in his 'No Bells and Whistles' repertoire: the two-hander, *Tuesdays with Morrie*, and four one-man performances: *A Night with the Stars, The Gospel of St. Mark, Spoken Treasures, and Sharing Shakespeare.*

He is an inspiration to all who know him or see his performances, and he is still promoting new ideas, trying new plays and learning new parts.

Despite his aging body, Antony's mind is as youthful today as it was in December 1939, when he stood in the spotlight at London's Royal Albert Hall to perform alongside the great American singer, Paul Robeson, or the day, two years later, when he stepped onstage at The Royal Cairo Opera House to direct and star in his signature piece, Emlyn Williams' play, *Night Must Fall.*

So, how does Antony view his first ninety years?

If he had the opportunity to remake his life he would probably not have married at such a young age and would have concentrated on furthering his career in London's West End, (although he is somewhat ambivalent on this point). However, he is absolutely adamant that he would not have married Catherine, his second wife.

He resents the time that he now has to spend on himself; the need to eat and drink at regular times; the care he has to take to avoid certain foods that disagree with him. Fortunately, he is still able to enjoy his favourite food – ice-cream, (but he will only eat the best).

He takes great pleasure in the fact that he can still work and still enjoys dancing, despite an arthritic knee which makes walking difficult at times. And he is proud of the fact that he is the oldest regularly working actor performing leading roles in North America – beating Mickey Rooney by exactly six months.

His most vivid memory is of the moment on Sunday, September 3, 1939, when he went to meet his girlfriend, Brenda Pool, on Primrose Hill in London, and found a note pinned to a tree saying she had gone home to hear the Prime Minister, Neville Chamberlain, speak on the radio. That moment marked the beginning of the Second World War and the best moment of Antony's life was in Cairo two years later when he sat chatting to Sir Claude Auchinleck in the inner sanctum of the Commander-in-Chief's office.

In real life, Antony's heroes include the 'greatest' names of twentieth century British theatre, Sir Laurence Olivier and Sir John Gielgud, but his greatest hero in history is the Roman Emperor Marcus Aurelius who ruled as the last of the 'Five Good Emperors' from 161-

180ce. and is recognized for his Stoic philosophy. Aurelius' teachings, known as *Meditations*, have numerous references to the theatre and include many homilies that resonate with Antony, such as: 'Natural ability without education has more often raised a man to glory than education without natural ability'

On the subject of talent versus training, Antony points to Emma Thompson, the eldest daughter of his Bristol Old Vic student and friend, Phyllida Law. Emma is an Academy Award winner and is one of the world's best known leading actresses, both in the movies and on the stage, yet she did not attend theatre school. So Antony's advice to any youngster who wants to become an actor today is, "Just go for it".

Despite Antony's documented disadvantages as a young actor, it is difficult to understand why someone with such talent and passion for his calling did not become a megastar. "I just lost the ambition somewhere along the road," he says. "I guess I wasn't willing to do what it takes."

As for Antony's complicated, and at times disastrous, personal life, perhaps it is best left to family members to explain. In the words of his daughter, Rosheen: "He has embraced his life and has always accepted his lot and made the best of it. He was, and still is, addicted to the stage, and Mum enabled him to follow his passion despite the hardships. Maybe she shouldn't have done. Maybe she should have put her foot down and told him to get a real job. He couldn't have done it without her."

Antony's granddaughter, Jasmine, adds, "I am well aware that all families have complications and there can often been a great deal of pain and sorrow. My fondest memory was when my husband and our three children along with my sister, her husband and their two children, and my mother and father all went to (aunt) Rosheen and Bob's farm and my grandmother (Gusta) and grandfather (Antony) were there as well. It was a truly splendid day in the sunshine and if you saw the photos you would never know the history of our family as we all look so happy together."

As we mourn the passing of the last surviving servicemen from the First World War we are already witnessing the demise of the next generation of heroes – the men and women who rid Europe of fascism in the 1940s. It is more than seventy years since the start of World War II and most of those lucky enough to survive the hostilities are now in their graves. All too soon we will be saluting the last of these brave souls and it's a fair bet that Antony Holland, a veteran of the North Africa Campaign, will be among them.

No one should be surprised to learn that Antony's chosen epitaph would be: Antony Holland – *An actor to the last.*

· But, perhaps the final words should go to William Shakespeare, who could have been writing of Antony Holland when he gave Griffith in *Henry VIII* the lines:

> Though from a humble stock, undoubtedly
> Was fashion'd to much honour from his cradle.
> He was a scholar, and a ripe and good one;
> Exceeding wise, fair-spoken, and persuading:
> Lofty and sour to them that loved him not;
> But, to those men that sought him, sweet as summer.

The End
(Applause)

Appendices

Directing (Selected Credits)

The Adding Machine

The Antique Bandit

Arms and the Man

Arsenic and Old Lace

Absent Friends

A Christmas Carol

Absurd Person Singular

Alice in Wonderland

A Pound on Demand

A Doll's House

A Penny for a Song

Boy Meets Girl

Blithe Spirit

Black Chiffon

The Browning Version

The Case of the Frightened Lady

The Case of the Left-Handed
Corpse

Charley's Aunt

The Cherry Orchard

Confusions

The Corn is Green

The Dark Side of Christopher
Malrose

The Doctor in Spite of Himself

The Duck Variations

Duet for Two Hands

Equus

Easy Money

Flare Path

Funny Peculiar

The Gathering

The Ghost Train

The Girl Who Couldn't Quite

Good

George Washington Slept Here

Harvey

Hamlet

Hamp

The Holly and the Ivy

How the Other Half Loves

Hobson's Choice

Harlinquinade

Hindle Wakes

The Imaginary Invalid

The Importance of Being Earnest

Intimate Exchanges

Journey's End

Juno and the Paycock

Just Between Ourselves

Jane Steps Out

Joking Apart

Ladies in Retirement

Lady Audley's Secret

The Lady's Not for Burning

The Last Case of Inspector Trent

The Linden Tree

The Lion of Heart

Love on the Sole

Macbeth

Major Barbara

The Miracle Worker

Mr. Roberts

Mrs. Warren's Profession

Night Must Fall

The Norman Conquests

Of Mice and Men

Oh What a Lovely War

On Approval

On Monday Next

Othello

Our Town

The Patsy

Peer Gynt

Playboy of the Western World

Present Laughter

Rattle of a Simple Man

Rebecca

The Rehearsal

Relatively Speaking

The Resistable Rise of Arturo II

Richard II

Richard III

Riders to the Sea

Rope

The Seagull

Season's Greetings

The Shop at Sly Corner

The Silver Box

Sisterly Feelings

The Sport of Kings

Squaring the Circle

Stalag 17

Stevie

That Championship Season

The Three Sisters

Thunder Rock

Tobias and the Angel

Tomorrow's Child

Top Girls

Treasure Island

Under Milkwood

Victoria Regina

Voyage Round my Father

Waiting for Godot

We the Undersigned

What the Butler Saw

While the Sun Shines

Whisper to Mendelsohn

Yossel's Music

You Can't Take it With You

You Know I Can't Hear You When the Water's Running

Acting and Performance (Selected Credits)

The Adding Machine

All My Sons

Androcles and the Lion

Angels in Love

As You Like It

The Bald Soprano

Better Watch Out – Better Not Die

The Biko Inquest

Black Apples

Black Limelight

The Browning Version

The Case of the Frightened Lady

Charley's Aunt

The Caine Mutiny Court Marshall

The Caretaker

A Child's Christmas in Wales

A Christmas Carol

The Collection

The Corn is Green

The Country Wife

The Critic

The Crucible

The Cut-Off

Dangerous Corner

The Deep Blue Sea

A Delicate Balance

The Dover Road

The Dumb Waiter

Eden End

Family Matters

The Flashing Stream

The Flying Squad

Fortune and Men's Eyes

French Without Tears

Gas Works

George and Margaret

The Ghost Train

Good Friday

The Gospel According to St. Mark

Granny Had a Little Gun

Halfway Up a Tree

Hamlet

The Happiest Days of Your Life

Harvey

Heartbreak House

Henry V

Hobson's Choice

Home

The Hostage

The House of Blue Leaves

I Have Been Here Before

The Importance of Being Earnest

In Celebration

Intimate Exchanges

Isadore and G.B.

Jack and the Beanstalk

Julius Caesar

The Killing of Sister George

King Lear

The Knack

Lady Audley's Secret

Larkrise to Candleford

The Late Christopher Bean

The Lesson

The Light of Heart

Little Murders

The Long and the Short and the Tall

Long Day's Journey into Night

Look for the White

Love Letters

The Love of Four Colonels

Macbeth

The Man of Destiny

The Man Who Came to Dinner

The Merchant of Venice

Mother Goose

Mountain Air

The Mousetrap

Mystery Play of the Nativity

Next Time I'll Sing to You

Night Must Fall

The Night of the Iguana

A Night with the Stars

No Man's Land

Nothing Sacred

Othello

Our Town

Peasants in Revolt

Philadelphia Here I Come

Poetry as Entertainment

Richard II

Richard III

The Raft

The Real Inspector Hound

Romeo and Juliet

The Room

Rope

Roundabout

Ruined by the BBC

Saint Joan

The Sea

Sharing Shakespeare

She Stoops to Conquer

The Sleeping Clergyman

Sweet Home

Ten Little Indians

The Taming of the Shrew

Time and Again

The Times Table

Tomorrow's Child

The Torchbearers

Trespass

Tuesdays with Morrie

Under Milkwood

Village Wooing

Yes and No

You Can't Take it With You

Film & Television (Selected Credits)

The Accused

Amber & Nichole

A Piano for Mrs. Cimino

Assault and Matrimony

Backfire

Battlestar Galactica

Beachcombers (3 episodes)

The Best Christmas Pageant Ever

Bill and Ted's Excellent
Adventure

Bingo

Captain 'n The Game Master

The Chris Isaak Show (3 episodes)

Christmas Comes to Willow
Creek

Christmas Star

Cobra

Cousins

Danger Bay (2 episodes)

Deadly Intentions

Deadly Intentions Again

Earthsea

Eureka

Escape

The Glitter Dome

Grey Fox

He-Man

Highlander

Hands of a Stranger

High Stakes

The Hitchhiker

Housekeeping

How to Break a Quarter Horse

Impolite

Kingdom Hospital

Last of the Dog-Men

Just Another Missing Kid

K-2

Legends of the Fall

Macgyver

The Manipulators (3 episodes)

The Man Who Wouldn't Die

McCabe and Mrs. Miller

Megan and the Ghosts

Mother Love

Mrs. Delafield Wants to Marry

Murphy's Law

Nancy Drew

Narrow Margin

National Lampoon's -
Thanksgiving Family Reunion

Neon at Night

Nellie, Daniel, Emma, Ben

Nobody's Child/The Marie Balter
Story

The Penthouse

Return of the Shaggy Dog

Sally Fieldgood and Company

Shattered Vows

Strange Luck

Supernatural

Survival on the Mountain

This Wouldn't Happen in Sarabar

Twelve Days of Christmas Eve

Twenty-One Jump Street,

We're No Angels

Wings

Wiseguy

Yes Virginia, There is a Santa Claus

You're Not Alone

Medals and Awards

<u>World War II</u>

      Defence Medal

      Battle of Britain Star

      39/45 War Medal

      British 8th Army – Africa Star

<u>Theatrical Awards</u>

Named 'Theatre Person of the Year" by the Vancouver Sun	1976
Nominated for ACTRA Best Actor Award for Shylock in CBC's Merchant of Venice	1977
Sam Payne Award for Humanity, Integrity and the Encouragement of New Talent	1985
Jessie Award - Best Performance-Lead Actor in Family Matters	1985
Jessie Award - Lifetime Achievement	1990
Union of BC Performers' Award of Excellence	2003
Elected to the BC Hall of Fame	2004
Jessie Award – Outstanding Performance in a Lead Role, (Morrie Swartz)	2007

About the Author

James Hawkins is a retired British police commander who has lived in Canada since 1989. Among other appointments, he was the Director of Education at The Canadian Institute for Environmental Investigations in Toronto from 1992-1997.
He is a multi-disciplinary author and playwright and his published works currently in print include:

Non-Fiction

The Canadian Private Investigators Manual (D.James Hawkins).
Published by Emond Montgomery and Canada Law Books, Toronto. (1996 – 2nd Ed.2002)

1001 Fundraising Ideas & Strategies for Charity (Jim Hawkins).
Published by Fitzhenry & Whiteside, Toronto (1997)

Eileen Wilson – Still Dancing at 90 (Biography)
Published by Bliss Publications, Gabriola, BC. (2009)

Fiction
Published by The Dundurn Group, Toronto/London and New York.

Missing: Presumed Dead *(2001 – Reprint 2011) (Finalist – Best First Novel 2001)*
The Fish Kisser *(2001)*
No Cherubs for Melanie *(2002)*
A Year Less a Day *(2002)*
The Dave Bliss Quintet *(2003)*
Lovelace & Button (International Investigators) Inc. *(2004)*
Crazy Lady *(2005)*
Deadly Sin *(2006)*

NB. All the above novels are available as eBooks from Kobobooks

Stage Plays
(Published by Bliss Publications)

No Cherubs for Melanie *(2011) (First performed 2001)*

The Dave Bliss Quintet – In Performance *(2011) (First performed at John Bassett Theatre, Toronto- 2004)*

Forthcoming Stage Play (August 2012)
Antony's Private Parts - Exposed